How to make
your business
work for you

THE SECRETS OF SUCCESS

For Busy Entrepreneurs and Executives

Brian James

and

Philip Crowshaw

How to Make your Business Work for you
Copyright © 2008 by Brian P James and Philip Crowshaw

ISBN 13: 978-0-9548916-2-6

Bonus Chapters Copyright © Doug Hills , Catherine Carthy, Alan Coulson, Andy Fogg and Penny Lowe

Graphic design by Farr Out Publications

"This seminal book, *How to make your business work for you* shows astonishing credibility. It's packed from start to finish with sound principles, insights and techniques. Every page is a 'call to arms', with well-researched and immediately practical guidelines for concentrating your thoughts and emotions, and an invitation to work towards your most resourceful business goals."
Max Eames—author of "Wealth Mechanic"

"*How to make your business work for you* is an accessible and engaging read. Clear and straightforward examples are used throughout to demonstrate the all important difference between surviving and thriving in business today. If you are fed up with scraping by and want to take your business to the next level, a copy of this book should be required reading."
Gill Pritchard, Just Add Content

"I just had to write to say thank you for the words of wisdom spoken during your recent workshops. I can honestly say that they have helped me become more successful, more satisfied and, strangely enough, more relaxed.

I've put into action some of the ideas that you have put forward and these are helping me to improve and grow my business.

Some of the ideas may seem so obvious, such as Managing your Resources:

Managing your resources requires ruthless prioritisation of tasks within your three key resource areas of important daily, weekly and monthly tasks.

Having recently set up my own business, I've come to realise how important these simple yet essential tasks are.

Both in running the business and in achieving satisfaction on a daily basis for tasks completed.

On a wider point, keeping a sensible work-life balance is important for me too, I have been given some life-changing thoughts that I will never forget about how our minds work and on life in general.

About our life's journey we were told:

The most important thing is to keep moving on your journey. There is no time for standing still.

And:

Throw out indecision and procrastination— the thieves of time and opportunity.

How true.

I too am a strong believer in the PMA (positive mental attitude) and find this helps on an every-day basis, helping to set and achieve goals and complete tasks successfully and in a timely fashion. These are only a few of the tips I've gained from these workshops, I'm really looking forward to getting my copy of the new book *Don't Work for your Business – Make your Business Work for You."*

Robert Hughes, Photographer & Engineering Designer

"There are many business books that purport to extol wisdom that the business person (whether new or experienced) cannot possibly do without. Few live up to their claims. This one does. And it does it in a lively and interesting style—not at all stuffy, boring 'hard to keep awake' prose that does nothing to inspire or motivate you. It takes you from setting your own personal and business goals through to managing customer relationships—complete with sample questionnaires, creating an effective team in your organisation, creating the right strategies for your business and much more.

Case studies and stories are used to illuminate and demonstrate the points being made in the book—that's what makes it so interesting—I particularly like the story on page 42—it so clearly describes how we can sabotage our businesses before we even get started!

Take the time to read this book (it's so easy to read)—you will gather many gems that will help you build your own successful business, both from a practical and mindset angle."

Carol Bentley, author of "I Want to Buy Your Product... Have You Sent me a Letter Yet?"

"A very readable business guide with great stories and case studies to bring the theory alive and make it easier to understand and act upon. This book is aimed at those who are committed to making their businesses truly successful."

Linda Denny, Smart Coaching Co

"This book is awesome! It's highly practical. Covers a lot of critical areas including Time Management, Decision Making, Team Work, highly effective direct marketing techniques, customer relationships and it even helps you come up with a powerful USP! As the title implies, as business owners we need to make the transition from working for our businesses to having our businesses work for us. This book can help you do that. And the bonus chapters are excellent. I always recommend this book to every serious entrepreneur I meet."

Edward Rivis, author of "Ultimate Web Strategy"

"One of the most practical and readable business books I've found. The vision of an effective company that works for the owner, employees and customers is compelling.

The book is very comprehensive, covering all areas of business from planning to sales. I was particularly impressed with the chapter on customer relationships. Customer management is a field I'd worked in myself for many years and I'd got rather complacent about it. The fresh viewpoint and positive approach fired me up to review our processes and see how we could do better.

If you want to take a new look at your company, improve your processes or get a better vision of what you're trying to achieve, I would certainly recommend this book. It has joined my shelf of much-thumbed reference books."
Anne Currie of Working Progam

Bringing it all together

The methods and principles suggested in this book are all tried and tested. They are all known to work and to produce substantial improvements if applied appropriately and consistently. Each method is powerful on its own, yet combined; the methods provide scope for massive profitable returns.

Your business has the inherent capability of growing to whatever size you want it to be. This can provide you with a wonderful lifestyle, a feeling of accomplishment, personal recognition and the opportunity to leave a legacy. There is no other more powerful vehicle for achieving growth and prosperity. This is yours to claim—don't waste it. You can secure ongoing and even greater business success. Go and claim it.

Check out the free resources available online at www.brianjamesgroup.com.

Bonus offer worth £50 when you buy this book
www.expertsonline.tv is the world's leading online Business TV Channel for people interested in Business and Personal Development and you get a free one year subscription worth £50 when you buy this book.

Whether you are a budding entrepreneur preparing to start your business for the first time or you're an established small business looking to grow, we have all the information and inspiration you need to be successful.

Our extensive range of unique TV programmes, with additional bonus audio and text based content, will support you in your journey to greater success. Across the site you'll find information and inspiration on Business Growth,

Finance, Sales, Marketing, Business Planning, HR, IT, Legal and many other business areas.

See and hear interviews with leading experts, including: Anita Roddick, Charles Handy, Sir John Harvey Jones, Simon Woodroffe, Rosemary Conley, Kriss Akabusi, Rachel Elnaugh, Duncan Bannatyne, Nigel Risner, Max Clifford and many, many more—in fact new content is added every week.

Just send us an e-mail to info@expertsonline.tv quoting the ISBN number of this book and where you bought it from to claim your free one year subscription worth £50 to Expertsonline.tv—you won't be disappointed!

About
Brian James

Brian James is creator of the breakthrough Triple M™ marketing methodology and founder of the Sales & Marketing Academy, a membership programme for ambitious business owners and managers providing ongoing advice, coaching and mentoring support.

Brian has been interviewed on national television as a business authority and has worked with blue-chip and small to medium sized companies across many sectors.

Some of the larger organisations he has worked with include the Prudential Group and British Telecom.

He currently operates as Chairman of the Brian James Group, a business advisory Group for owner managed businesses.

About
Philip Crowshaw

Philip Crowshaw is the founder of the globally acclaimed online business TV channel www.expertsonline.tv. He is passionate about helping people to achieve their full potential by developing their ability to think the right things in the right way. Philip is also the developer of the 'Blue Print of Success' system which is taught to people around the world to help them achieve their business and life goals.

As Managing Director of Experts Group, Philip works to design and deliver business improvement programmes and online resources for people and organisations seeking to be better at what they do.

Background Research to this Book
In 2003, after a successful corporate career with organisations such as Phone 4 U and Thomas Cook, Philip started out on his own by undertaking hundreds of hours of research, including filming over 150 high profile successful people, with a view to identifying if there was a pattern to achieving greater business success.

This book captures the conclusions made from that research, including transcripts from the actual video interviews with the rich and famous talking about their life journey and how they achieved their success.

Over 18 months, supported by business guru Brian James, Philip and Brian studied a wide variety of people, who had been nominated by others, to identify how they had achieved large and small successes. The research data was collated and analysed, culminating in the information described in this book.

Although the research and development was conducted in the UK, the learning elements have no national boundaries.

This book is different from anything else you have ever seen before; buyers of the book can get free online access to the actual video interviews conducted for the book, along with a wide range of other video, audio and text based resources to help you become more successful.

Just send an e-mail to us at info@expertsonline.tv including the ISBN number of the book with the shop name and location to claim your free one year subscription.

Contents

Chapter 1

Maximising business growth

"The only certain means of success is to render more and better service than is expected of you, no matter what your task may be." — Og Mandino

Small to medium enterprise (SME) businesses face many challenges today if they are to survive and thrive. You have selected this book presumably because you want to be not just one of the survivors — you want to create lifestyle, financial independence and take control of your working and personal life. There is no better way of achieving this than by running a successful business.

Statistically, the odds are against you, as you probably already know. It is common knowledge that the majority of businesses fail within the first few years; typically 80% within five years. According to a recent survey* 50,000 firms are set to fold over the next two years. When you consider all the effort, risk and passion that goes into starting a business, this is a sad revelation and, in my view, it is avoidable.

So where do most business owners go wrong? There are two key reasons for business failure. Interestingly, they are linked to the market economy but in many cases, they are self-induced. The two key reasons are:

1. Failure to take appropriate advice
2. Unwillingness to adapt to change

Running a successful business is a complex matter and it is no surprise that goals are often not achieved. Stress, chaos, overwork and constant fire fighting are the hallmarks of many businesses today. Of course, it doesn't have to be this way, but just for now let's consider some of the root causes of this adverse situation.

*From BDO Stoy Hayward survey, based on DTI figures.

Whilst you attempt to deliver your unique market proposition through your defined product, service or treatment offering, you are confronted with a myriad of issues to resolve. The issues have to be managed on a daily basis. Here are some of them, listed in three categories.

Financial Management
- Business plans
- Financing arrangements
- Cash-flow forecasts
- Profit and loss statements
- Credit control
- Budgeting
- Profit testing
- Taxation
- Auditing

Process Management
- I.T. Systems
- Business premises
- Processes and Procedures
- Quality control (ISO 9000)
- Business insurance
- Company vehicles
- Plant and Equipment requirements
- Customer development
- Customer service
- Stock requirements

People Management
- Recruitment
- Motivation
- Training and Development
- Communication
- Roles and Responsibilities
- Employment law
- Health and Safety requirements
- Life and Pension schemes
- Staff policy, compensation and benefits
- Investors in People awards

- Employee relations
- Organisational design

It is certainly a tall order to manage all these elements. It takes creativity and highly organised practise on an ongoing basis. Despite the challenges, it is possible and highly achievable to actually make it work. It requires a number of essential elements.

Business owners need laser-like focus on where they are heading with detailed, documented plans. Procedures need to be in place that everyone in the business can work to. This makes a business rely more upon systems than on people. Good people are of course essential. Human nature being as it is, people can be unreliable. Quality systems can help compensate for this situation. Roles and responsibilities need to be clearly defined, empowering people and making them accountable. Quality two-way communication is essential at all levels.

The survival and success factors

This book seeks to share core principles that can create dynamic and immediate growth in your business. It provides concrete methods to increase your customers and maximise profitability from your existing customer base. You will be given practical tips to use in the effective systemisation of your business and offered help with key people management issues

In order to survive you need to maintain two factors. *You need to be able to sustain a profit and you need to produce results for customers.* Once you have demonstrated to the market place that you can produce tangible results for your customers and you can retain a profit, then there is no reason for your business ever to fail. This is of course assuming that the business operates with integrity and is compliant. This can offer some reassurance. Your business can be sustained by applying simple principles. This requires being prepared to change as the market changes and seeking the appropriate professional advice when needed.

Beyond basic survival and sustaining factors, I hope you want to maximise your business potential and grasp opportunities to the full for profitable growth. This also requires two key factors. Firstly, innovation can help, although this is usually short lived once competitors start to catch up. Secondly, effective marketing on a vigorous and ongoing basis is essential. The rest of this book focuses on numerous tried and tested marketing strategies and formulæ that will work if applied progressively and systematically.

---

*Apply effective marketing on a
vigorous and ongoing basis.*

As a management consultant I have witnessed many examples of huge successes and spectacular failures. Take the financial services company that was a fledgling business with three partners turning over less than £500,000. We worked with them for 18 months to help grow their distribution. They had great plans and a visionary outlook. In less than three years of consistently applying proven methods, they had transformed into a national organisation, £10 million turnover and were employing dozens of staff. You can achieve similar or greater levels of success with the right mindset and by consistently applying methods that are proven to work.

The dimensions of business success thinking

Because businesses involve people, they operate as a microcosm of the living world. Every business is unique. This is because it is made up of the efforts, desires and personalities of a collection of unique individuals.

Most business owners focus on the "here and now". They concentrate on the immediate demands of a delivery cycle. This involves securing orders, producing goods or services and delivering or distributing them. This is purely demand led and does not lead to any creative thought or development.

It is neither reflective nor insightful. It becomes extremely monotonous and a stifling environment to work in. It will certainly not enable the full potential to be realised.

Success thinking, on the other hand, involves a much broader context. It involves considering the full dynamics of the business, from its past roots through to its current state and projected in to future possibilities. The past, the future and the present are all equally important and omnipotent. To capture vital information from the past requires systemised recording. Creating a shared vision of the future requires documented planning.

The future and effective planning

Business planning will be covered in more depth in later chapters. For now, however, a brief overview will help to set the scene. Every journey starts with the destination in mind. It is constantly amazing that many people spend more time planning their annual holiday than their personal and business lives. How ludicrous it would be, when seated on a 'plane just before take-off if the Captain made the following announcement: "Good morning everyone. This is flight 410. As it's a nice day I thought it would be interesting to just take off and fly somewhere different. I don't know where yet but I thought it would be fun to explore somewhere new. We could end up anywhere. Isn't this fun?".

Can you imagine it? The passengers would want to get off the 'plane very fast. It's an obvious point: however, so many business owners overlook the essential steps of recognising when they have arrived at a successful outcome.

The steps include the following:
- Start with an open mind to the true potential of your business. Every business has the inherent capability of producing outstanding profitability and astonishing results for customers.
- Think big. Imagine what you would strive to achieve if you knew you couldn't fail. Develop the mindset that nothing is totally impossible. Sometimes there are only

unrealistic timescales. Consider some of the incredible technological breakthroughs over the last century. The personal computer is one obvious example that in recent history could have only been a dream.

- Match and track your activities to your objectives on a daily basis. Work with passion and a laser-like focus with persistency and consistency. Success thinkers and achievers are great visionaries. We can all be visionary by working in our areas of true passion. It took fourteen years of persistence for Albert Einstein's Theory of Relativity to become officially recognised. Don't expect instant success.

The past and systemisation

You can create significant competitive advantage by learning from the past and using the experience gained to modify methods and behaviours. Do not make the error, however, of living on past glories or dwelling on previous mistakes. The past becomes a point of reference, not a place of residence! Monitoring and refining enables you to implement ongoing improvements to your business operation. You can make your business *system-reliant* rather than *people-reliant*. Systemisation does not mean your people are any less valuable. On the contrary, your people must be recognised and valued. People prefer to work in an environment of understanding and known expectations. Operating within quality systems can achieve this for you and enable you to reward the performance of your people.

Make your business system-reliant rather than people-reliant.

Monitor every activity your business and staff perform. Keep detailed records and reward performance. Make people accountable for their actions and their performance. Accountability does not mean looking for someone to blame when something goes wrong. It is a learning culture rather than a blaming culture.

There are finite reasons why desired outcomes are not achieved:

- The system is flawed and is in need of refinement
- The people involved are not operating the system correctly

The solution then becomes a combination of the following:

- Review and refine the system or create a new system
- Retrain the people using the system

You may continue to suffer from repetitive failures in the use of the system by certain individuals. This is because they have not been adequately trained or they are not capable of performing that function to the required standard. Further training may help; otherwise consider offering them a role more suited to their talents. Everyone has areas of key interest where they can excel. Find out what these are and allow people to work to their strengths. They will be far more motivated and will perform at a consistently higher level. It is very rare that people fail for fun. On the whole people like to perform well, achieving recognition and due reward for their efforts.

On the whole, people like to perform well, achieving recognition and due reward for their efforts.

People management checklist

- Sketch out your current organisational structure
- Predict the structure you need in order to achieve your vision
- Create a job description and key responsibilities for every role

- Work with people's strengths in order to achieve maximum harmony and effectiveness
- Invest in your people to refine their skills
- Demand performance and make people accountable for results
- Give people the freedom to be empowered
- Insist on learning not blaming culture

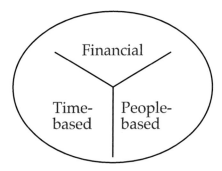

How well are you managing your three key business resources?

Managing your resources

This requires ruthless prioritisation of tasks within your three key resource areas. These resources are financial, time-based and people-based. The priorities will include important daily, weekly, monthly and other functions that need to be performed on a regular and consistent basis. This information needs to be communicated to your people so they can take responsibility for their role.

The following is an example checklist of regular tasks:

Daily tasks:
- Diary management
- Customer contact

Weekly tasks:
- Invoicing
- Credit control

Monthly tasks:
- Planning
- Budgeting

Record time spent on each activity:
- Prospecting
- Customer fulfilment
- Administration

Controlling your environment

There are two environments within your business. They are your *external* environment and your *internal* environment. Your external environment includes aspects such as market size, geo-demographics, legal requirements and market trends. While you cannot control these factors directly, you can choose those markets that you operate within. You can learn to understand your markets and predict them. You can control how you respond to external changes and pressures.

You can learn to understand your markets and predict them. You can control how you respond to external changes and pressures.

You do have control over your internal environment. You have the power to choose the operating and marketing methods that best suit your business. The success of this is completely in your hands. You choose the level of resource you apply to grow and manage your business. You are able to influence your chosen markets directly through the marketing and customer fulfilment methods you adopt. The success of your marketing will be dependent upon factors such as how well you focus on your target markets, how well you test to minimise risk and how effective your communications are to maximise an immediate positive response.

Case study: Two similar businesses producing vastly different results

Both businesses operate in wholesale distribution and are located within the same geographic area.

	Business 1	**Business 2**
No of owners	2	3
Time in business	10 years	8 years
Marketing methods	• Field sales • Direct mail	• Tele sales • Direct mail • Exhibitions • Alliance partnerships • Loyalty programmes
Level of systemisation	• Accounting • Order taking and delivery	• Highly systemised throughout operation
Turnover	£1M	£10M
Profitability	20%	10%

Results for the business owners

	Business 1	**Business 2**
Profit per business owner (NPBT*)	£100,000	£333,000

* Net profit before tax

For Business 2, the owners have over three times the level of annual profits. There are many factors involved: however, there are two key reasons for this. Business 2 has more effective marketing and more efficient use of systems.

Building existing customer value

Understanding and maintaining customer expectations is a key requirement. Your customers will stay loyal while you are delivering results, known expectations and offering greater value.

---

*Your customers will stay loyal
while you are delivering results,
known expectations and offering
greater value.*

It costs typically four to nine times more to acquire new customers compared with retaining existing customers. While it is always essential to continue to grow your customer base you will also want to maximise the return from existing customers. By ensuring that your customers are continually receiving greater value from you, it is axiomatic that you will receive greater value from them. This includes recognising the lifetime value of customers plus taking advantage of up-selling, cross-selling and back-end selling opportunities. Maximising customer referral opportunities and developing alliance partnerships with select customers are other indispensable elements. These will be covered in detail in a later chapter.

Using creativity for effective decision-making

A successful business leader is a decision making machine. Creative decision-making injects new ideas into the decision making process. You are able to evaluate options that may not have been considered previously. This encourages innovative thought and broadens people's perspective to discover better solutions. It is also a way of injecting fun into what may otherwise be a routine task.

---

*A successful business leader is a
decision-making machine.*

The precedent versus innovation argument challenges the traditional route that may have always been followed in the past. In favour of tradition, we have proven, tried and tested methods. On the other hand, traditional methods may be resource-intensive and ineffective. We need to keep abreast of current methods, technologies and expectations that change over time.

Here is a checklist for introducing and encouraging creative ideas

- Ask for and circulate ideas from others
- Be prepared to take manageable risk
- Test possible options
- Obtain feedback and gauge acceptability levels from others
- Avoid leaving too much to chance!
- Link ideas to long-term plans
- Be decisive

Making lists and involving others where possible can achieve the requirements for gathering and assessing relevant information. The use of mind mapping and other prioritisation techniques can help. Ensure timescales are realistic. Complex problems can be broken down into more manageable steps.

Overall, creativity adds openness and flexibility to the decision-making process. Costs and resources need to be managed carefully. Ultimately, this can produce better solutions and more buy-in from others. Outcomes need to be justified based on more effective results.

Case Study: Innovation at work

A major financial services company established in the 1820s had challenges with increased competition and reduced margins due to increasing costs of compliance. They needed creative and innovative solutions to create competitive advantage. A new range of investment and protection products were developed taking advantage of special taxation benefits that were available in the UK. A European subsidiary was established in Dublin that promoted the products to the UK market. Within three years the subsidiary company generated in excess of ten percent of the combined business turnover which at that stage was around £2 billion per annum. This jettisoned the company into a position of substantially increased profitability and competitive advantage.

Managing key risks

Risk management is the process of identifying and controlling key risks that can damage your business. This includes sudden events like fire, flood or burglary as well as gradual decline such as poor staff retention rates, high customer attrition or ineffective financial management. The main benefits of sound risk management include:

- Greater business efficiency
- Reduced exposure to litigation
- Lower risk associated with costly, damaging and disruptive events

Your business is exposed to a complex range of risks that may be underestimated. Less than 25% of businesses operate reliable safety, security and personnel procedures. These risks all have the potential to cause severe damage to your business. Sound contingency planning and specialist support are crucial. The following areas identify where risk management is required to maintain the well being of your business:

- Contracts and employment law
- Health and safety
- Cash and credit control
- Financial protection
- Customer growth and attrition
- Premises, vehicle and environmental management
- IT security
- Disaster recovery

Your business is exposed to a complex range of risks that may be under-estimated. Sound contingency planning and specialist support are crucial.

Making it work for you

You have the power to create dynamic and immediate growth in your business. Combine the three dimensions of business growth whilst minimising risk. The three dimensions are effective planning, process and people management. Make your business accountable for its past, present and future. Combine multiple marketing strategies for finding, keeping and growing customers. You can innovate and educate your market place. Systemise every business operation with an ongoing process of refinement. Recognise and reward your people for performance. Get them working to their strengths. This is all part of becoming a decisive business leader and creating positive influence on others wherever you go.

Interview with
Rosemary Conley

What does success mean to Rosemary Conley?
I think I would say that the nicest thing about being successful is that people actually respect what you say, they actually respect your opinion. Until you become successful, then you're just a person out there along with everyone else. I'm sure there are lots of people out there who have much more wisdom than me and can say wonderful things, but success does bring you respect and that's nice.

You started out with very little money; what was your dream, your vision?
Well I had no dreams about a future or a working career for myself. I was born in 1946 and accordingly I thought you got married when you could; you had children and that was it, that was your lot really as a woman. The amazing thing was that when I first got married I'd put on a lot of weight and then I learned about calories and losing weight. I then thought 'wouldnt it be great to actually start a class'.

This was really the beginning of when classes were being held and so I got together a few neighbours and then they lost weight on a diet that I'd written and we decided to go to the local village hall. I had 30 posters printed which cost me £8 and that was the launch of my very first business.

But at that point I had no aspirations of where this might lead me and no idea that I might actually be quite good at it. I mean I'd gone through school, I left school at 15 and went to secretarial college. I even failed my shorthand exam. And so I wasn't somebody who had any confidence from an academic point of view. Suddenly I was standing up in front of this group of women, talking to them about how to lose weight and they were listening, and it worked, and when they came back the next week and they got on the scales and they'd lost weight, they were so excited! I was so excited!

For the first time in my life I actually felt I was doing something well and I felt good about it. My confidence grew from there, and then after a period of about eight years I was contacted by a national publishing company to run similar classes to my slimming classes, around Leicestershire, and would I do it nationally for them in association with a magazine. Now this was the interesting bit because I'd really enjoyed running this little cottage industry in Leicestershire and I'd got about ten girls working for me. It was a nice little business, fabulous. Suddenly I'm into the big business. I'm travelling to London and going to the board meetings with this big company and it was horrible, because it was all bottom line and I hadn't got the capability to really understand how it was all working; and of course a business has to be profitable, I understand that. But the biggest problem was that I was trying to do everything myself and I hadn't got the confidence to say, 'actually I need some help; I can't do everything'. Really I was doing that before my time. I was there for four years (I had a five year contract) and it was the worst four years of my life.

After such an experience, what's your advice to aspiring entrepreneurs?

I think you need to look at the opportunities that come along and weigh up what they are going to bring you. When I look back at those four years, it actually taught me a huge amount; first of all it brought me down with my feet on the ground fair and square, and I had to, in effect, start again. But it doesn't take you as long to build up to where you were before, the second time around. I've heard people say, 'if you lost everything in a fire tomorrow, you've lost everything except yourself'. It wouldn't take you so long to get back up to where you were because nobody can take away the experiences that you have learned. And so I would say, look at the opportunities but don't sell your soul. It's really important to be doing what you want to do and what you are naturally good at. After I'd gone through that experience I made sure that I would actually never work for anybody again, and that I would from then on always work for myself. I don't regret doing what I did because I did learn a lot from it.

You mentioned not having certain management skills early on. Is it imortant to find people who do have them?

You definitely need to find somebody with the skills to help you learn them. I surround myself now, and I've been in the business 33 years, but I surround myself with experts and that is how I can deliver the right information about diet, the right information about exercise. I can speak in high places, having checked what I am proposing to say. I mean, even the Prime Minister has everything he is proposing to say looked at. I have the confidence to go out there and actually deliver the words and not use notes and just speak it. I am happy to do that, but I know that I've got my facts straight from the experts. I am just about to launch a range of food in the very near future. As the manufacturer sends me through the data, I send it through to my nutrition scientist to check and ask her opinion and what's the general public's opinion of this additive or this nutrient or whatever. Is it going to do what it says it's going to do? And this is extra high in this good nutrient, can we make a claim about this nutrient? So I check all those things, and it's swallowing pride and realising that you don't have to be good at everything.

Did you also hit financial setbacks?

The worst was the loss of the salary when the clubs that I was running for this national company were to be disbanded. Suddenly my executive salary and the executive car went, and at that point I was just literally running a few of my own classes, and my husband (well he wasn't my husband then but he became my husband six months later) was out of a job as well so we were, in effect, living on very little at that time.

What did that teach you?

Well I tell you what, it teaches you the value of money and you never, ever forget it, no matter how much you've got. I've been very, very fortunate in the last 17 years since my Hip and Thigh Diet was such a huge success. My career took off then and I always look upon it as if the previous 15 years were like my apprenticeship so that when I did hit the big time, I knew what to do, I knew how to make it go forward, I knew how to grow the business and I had that experience of a bit of television, I had the experience of a bit of radio and I had the experience of tough times and difficult questions. When you've learned through those things, then being frightened by something like that isn't horrible, it's just scary and it's actually quite exciting.

We tend to assume that successful people don't have setbacks. What was your reaction when it happened to you?

Well, you learn by It. I was giving a talk to some schools the other day for a Young Enterprise Initiative, and I was saying, 'if life was easy, it wouldn't be fun'. It's because it's tough that when it comes out well the other side you so appreciate it. You'd think it would be dead easy if every athlete just went and won everything; what would be the satisfaction in that? I don't want to win the lottery; it's much too easy. I'd much rather have the success that I've had and feel that I've earned it. My husband and I feel the same. My husband has worked with me in my business and we feel enormous satisfaction in having done what we've done rather than it just be given to you on a plate.

In the current dietary debate, is there a lot of misinformation being passed on?

I'll address the misinformation thing first and then I'll come to the global epidemic of obesity (it's quite a trip).

One of the biggest worries that I have is that anything can be printed in any magazine and often is, and so you will open a newspaper and it will suddenly say, 'eat this fruit, eat this vegetable and it will cure this and it will prevent that'. Nobody has any clinical proof that that they are the facts. And so you get somebody who is interested in cosmetics suddenly doing this piece about, oh, this cream does this, this and this—they don't. And so there is an awful lot of rubbish written and that really frustrates me. This is why I've created our own magazine so that what we put in *Rosemary Conley Magazine* is actually ethically correct, it's proven, it's right and that's where we come from. That has its rewards, because people respect you for the fact that you don't just say any old thing.

But on the global question, it's a massive problem. I believe the Government is actually doing a lot more than any other Government has ever done before. My frustration comes in that there are lots of different committees, lots of good intentioned people trying to do things and there isn't one governing body that's drawing all those people together to say, 'actually, these are the initiatives that we need to do'.

So I get frustrated that there is lots of energy being spent trying to make it happen, but it won't happen until you get a central coordination. There are lots of good messages getting out there, and people are more aware that actually obesity is a problem.

Obesity can actually make you ill, it's not just about not fitting into your clothes. I'm even wearing my little pedometer here, to count my steps. I sold 20,000 of these, so people are actually getting the message that steps and activity do count. These are the messages that should be getting across but in a unified way.

So the pedometer could tempt people away from cars, buses and taxis?

Absolutely; it really does make people think, 'oh I'll go upstairs, oh I'll do it now', and it does make you much more conscious and that's very, very good. I've spoken to various committees. I've spoken in the House of Commons and I've spoken recently in the House of Lords and there are some good intentioned people there, but it's frustrating for all of them I think, that there isn't that central way of making it go forward.

Why are we not as physically active as we used to be?
Well I think there are two elements there; there is a competitive element where I think we're all becoming so politically correct and children shouldn't be put under this stress and that stress—for goodness sake, get a life! It really drives me nuts. Stress is what life is about and we can't be wrapped up in cotton wool, we have to face some really tough times, and yes, if somebody is better than you, then you can either try harder or give in—so, you know, you have those choices.

It really frustrates me that children are wrapped in cotton wool these days. If you want to get ahead, get out there and do something.

As far as activity is concerned, yes, children in schools are looking at computors much more. They are being less active and they are watching more television with so many television channels; yet again, I think this is really bad. I don't enjoy television as much now as I did, because I'm spoilt for choice and the whole quality seems to have been diluted. Children can find something that they want to watch. When children watch TV, they also want to eat. So their weight is going up through lack of activity and food consumption, whereas if they didn't watch television and they did activity, their weight would go down because there would be so many less calories. They would be spending more calories but taking fewer calories in, because they are not watching the television which is prompting them to eat. And so we need to restrict our television watching time and do more activity, and it will almost sort out the snacking bit.

What is your view of the fast food industry?

The fast-food industry is thriving because we have more disposable income. Go back to just after the war years, we wouldn't even dream about going and buying a burger even if it was there to go and have. You might go to the fish and chip shop on a Friday if you were lucky, but that was a treat. These days, we've only been hearing on the news this week to say that champagne sales in the UK are second only to France, and that heaven knows how many billion bottles of it we've consumed. Why? Because we can afford it. And because people can afford to buy food, they can afford to dine out more, they can afford to buy fast food, they can afford to drink more and, because they have more money, they have a car and don't have to walk so far. All of those things, it just makes activity less and consumption more, and this is where it goes wrong. We need to take responsibility for our bodies, we need to make choices. We were speaking at our local Council offices a year or eighteen months ago, it was at 12.00 noon. 120 people were in the room and I said, 'How many of you have eaten something at your desk this morning?' Over 100 of them had. That's what's making the country fat!

Is there a way of replacing the desire for fast food with a longing for better things?

It's education and it's discipline. I prefer to be slim. I know what it's like to be overweight. I hated it. I hated myself. I felt lousy, I couldn't sleep properly, my whole day was a torture as I fought for food and I made a choice and I learned. I programmed my brain over a period of time to condition it to not be so dependent upon food and to be disciplined and have only three meals a day. Everybody should have a breakfast, a lunch and a dinner and not eat in between. If you're not trying to lose weight and you just want to be healthy, if you must have something in between meals, have a piece of fruit. We can train ourselves—we can train ourselves to not go into that shop and steal something.

If we can do that, we can train ourselves not to eat the chocolate bar at 11.00am. We can do it, and if you want to be slim badly enough, you'll do it.

Do some overweight people eat the wrong foods as a comfort factor?

They seem to go for the very thing that they shouldn't be going for because it helps them to drown their sorrows, but very, very momentarily, and that is a real shame because it's like an alcoholic going for a drink: it doesn't solve the problem and we have to understand that. Part of the success that fortunately we have been able to achieve over the years, has been the fact that my confidence has grown as I've gained control of my weight and you are then able to use your brain cells in a much more constructive way to move your career forward and your life forward, to find happiness. Happiness is not eating food; some people think it is, but it's not, it's an artificial happiness.

You started with eight pounds and thirty posters. Did you ever imagine your business would grow so big?

Not a clue, not in my wildest dreams. It's lovely to be part of a business which changes people's lives. It's lovely to be part of a business that has so many departments, so to speak, because we have Rosemary Conley Diet and Fitness Clubs, which is a franchised operation, and that's been very successful and very exciting. Then we've got *Rosemary Conley Magazine*, which is published and out on sale on the high street. Then we've got my Rosemary Conley electrical products now, which are available in stores all over the land, so you can get your electric roaster or whatever, and that's all good stuff. Then we've got, obviously, my books and my videos are legendary—they've been around for a long time and I've sold a lot of them. So the chances are somebody has worked out with me in their lounge, which is quite exciting. I used to do a lot of telly; I don't do so much now. Now we're just about to go into food and new things keep coming, but I only do things that are fun.

So, building a business from scratch can still be done?
Absolutely. It's about finding out what you're good at. So try and find a career where you enjoy doing what you're doing, because if you're enjoying it, you're probably good at it and vice versa—so that makes a fundamental difference. I love every day that I wake up and go to work, I adore it—that's the first thing that you need to do.

The second thing is, you really want to have somebody you can share it with—find a friend who's been very good at it to be your mentor, to give you some tips and to point you in the right direction. The other thing is, you'll get much more satisfaction if what you do actually makes a difference to others, because there is this great feeling of worthwhileness. It's this feeling of actually, that's made that person feel happier. Now it doesn't matter whether you're a hairdresser and you're doing somebody's hair and they walk out of the salon feeling top notch, or whether you're a dress designer, whether you're somebody who paints nails or whatever it might be. If it's going to make somebody feel good because of what you've done, then that is fantastic.

Are there any books you would recommend to others?
There is a wonderful book by Rob Parsons, who is a Christian guy, who's a lawyer who wrote the book *The Key To Success*, and it is a fabulous read about not losing sight of the important things; your family life, getting your priorities right, getting the balance, getting the life/work balance correct. It's a fantastic book.

Richard Denny did a set of tapes. Richard Denny is a motivational guru, and they are called *Dare To Be Great*. They were key in my development. It made me realise that yes, by having the right attitude and having some goals, you could achieve so much more than you ever dreamt.

And then my third one would be *The Bible*. Read a bible; it will give you the best positive direction that you could ever, ever have. Stick to it and you can't go far wrong.

||||||||||||||||||||||||||||||||||||||||||||||||||||||||||||||||||||||||||||

Rosemary Conley is the UK's leading diet and fitness expert with over 35 years' experience of helping people lose weight and get fit.

In 1986 Rosemary discovered a low-fat diet plan, which transformed her body in a way she had never been able to achieve with previous diets.

Rosemary put her experiences down on paper and the result was her *Hip and Thigh Diet*, which was published in 1988 and captured the attention of the nation. This book and its sequel, *Rosemary Conley's Complete Hip and Thigh Diet*, have sold more than two million copies.Subsequent books and videos have seen similar spectacular success, despite being in such a highly competitive market place, with total worldwide sales fast approaching eight million.

||||||||||||||||||||||||||||||||||||||||||||||||||||||||||||||||||||||||||||

Watch this video interview plus many more like it through your free subscription to online business TV portal Expertsonline.tv available to you as a buyer of this book. Just send an e-mail to **info@expertsonline.tv**, *including the ISBN number, and the location of where you bought the book to receive your free subscription worth £50.*

Chapter 2

Personal goal setting

"Whether you think you will succeed, or not, you are right"
—Henry Ford

In order to reach your required destination for you, your people and your business, you need to set goals based on three dimensions. These are:

1. Individual personal goals
2. Business objectives
3. Aligned goals taking account of both individual and business objectives

Having spent a number of decades observing owner managers and business leaders, there are common elements that separate the great achievers from the rest.

In order to reach your true *business* potential you also have to aspire to certain *personal* beliefs and behaviours. These can be referred to as "success mind sets".

The great achievers have had and will always have a wealth of the following attributes:

1. An incredible sense of purpose and belief in a clear vision of the future
2. Being prepared to back their belief with laser-like focus on appropriate and highly disciplined consistent activity
3. Ability to combine intense focus with a balanced life
4. Being unstoppable in their quest for the success and achievement of their goals
5. Learning from great leaders and following tried and tested principles which have been proven to work
6. Totally committed to excellence and a lifetime of personal development

7. Using setbacks as learning opportunities not as excuses to give up
8. Thinking big; believing in their ability to make the impossible happen and become a reality
9. Maintaining a positive attitude
10. Believing in the power of working as a team for everyone to achieve more

Creating motivation for change

Have you ever thought about what will be said about your life when you are no longer part of this earth? What impression you will leave on the world? This can be envisioned by imagining that you are an observer at your own funeral. What is being said about you? What great things have you achieved? What lasting memories have you left in the minds of others? People may forget what others say, but they remember how they made them feel. Do you leave a positive impression on others? Do you encourage and inspire others to grow? What examples do you set for others to follow?

People may forget what others say, but they remember how they made them feel.

Your personal journey

If life is a journey and not a destination, then you are constantly travelling and moving towards your better life and away from the past. Along the way you will be meeting crossroads where you need to decide your chosen path. Some of the paths will be easy to see and perhaps worn from other frequent travellers. Some will be hidden from view and sometimes you will choose to make a new path of your own.

There will also be many roadblocks and barriers along your path that you have to overcome before moving on.

Sometimes roadblocks will be found that you can break through and other times you may decide to return back along your current path to find a new route. The most important thing is to keep moving on your journey. There is no time for standing still.

---

*The most important thing is to
keep moving on your journey.
There is no time for standing still.*

Taking constant and progressive action means sometimes falling short of your own quality standards. It is better to take action and do things badly at first, rather than expecting perfection and doing nothing. It takes time to create a masterpiece. X-rays reveal that Leonardo da Vinci painted Mona Lisa three other times beneath his final work. So don't expect instant results.

Your personal goals

You may not be where you want to be at the moment. You want to achieve more by way of:

- The things you want to *have*
- The things you want to *do*
- The person you want to *become*
- The people you want to *share* your life with

By having clear goals and a plan to follow you can move towards the life you really want and turn it into reality. You can be *pushed around* by your circumstances or *pulled forward* by your dreams. You choose!

Having a life mission

Finding a cause to live for is one of the most powerful forces known to mankind. Extraordinary results can be realised from ordinary people with a mission. This becomes your personal blueprint for achievement and creates an unstoppable mind set. I am happy to share my live mission with you if it helps you to find yours. "To live, to love, to learn, to lead and to leave a legacy."

Having established your mission, your plans and goals will provide the execution and logistics to carry them out.

The search for happiness

It is human nature to seek a better life, one of happiness and worthwhile achievement.

Happiness is that often elusive state of abundant pleasure.

Where are you on your happiness chart? As an exercise, scale yourself on the chart below from one to ten on both axes.

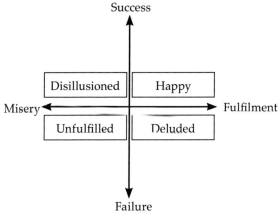

From despair to happiness

We all have our own view of what success means to us. For some it is financial success and independence. For others it is the quality of their relationships with others. You will have your version of what success means to you.

> *Fulfilment comes from
> accomplishment and
> contentment of spirit; by being
> stretched to the limit of your
> capacity but not beyond*

Fulfilment comes from accomplishment and contentment of spirit; by being stretched to the limit of your capacity, but not beyond. This is a sense of enjoyment and satisfaction for your efforts. Success and fulfilment need to be combined at a high enough level to create an overall feeling of satisfaction. This can create happiness, particularly if you feel gratitude as well for your current state. Not complacent, but appreciating where you are and being able to savour the moment. This involves recognising your achievements to date while still wanting more for the future.

Some people are incredibly successful from a personal wealth perspective but at the same time dreadfully unfulfilled. This is because they don't enjoy what they do or who they are. Others have an intense passion for who they are and what they do, yet consider themselves a complete failure. Maybe they have set unreasonable conditions on their levels of achievement. Maybe they seek a perfection that can never be reached.

Providing a balance
Maintaining a healthy balance is the key to ongoing and long-term well being. You can conduct the following exercise to assess your current levels of balance in your personal and business life. This can be referred to as the 7 Fs scale. Again, rate yourself from one to ten in each of the seven elements.

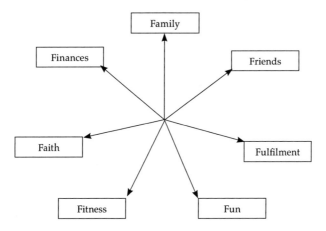

Your wheel of fortune on the 7 Fs scale

By being conscious of how well balanced your life is at any one time, you are able to reappraise your priorities. You are able to work towards greater enrichment and harmony. This adds to your overall well being.

When working towards a particular goal you may choose to be temporarily out of balance. For example, if you were training to run in a Marathon then it is likely that, for a period of time, your concentration would be towards gaining fitness whilst other parts of your life may be temporarily out of balance. This becomes a conscious trade-off.

Finding the true desires of your heart

We all have the inherent ability to achieve the true desires of our hearts. We can have an intense, focused burning desire to find and fulfil our unique purpose in life. There are exercises we can do to discover our true self and purpose. We can make a personal life assessment of ourselves at any one time. We can then decide what we want to implement to make the desired changes.

---

*We all have the inherent ability
to achieve the true desires of our
hearts.*

The origin of our true desires comes from several sources. These include our early childhood experiences when we encountered our first heroic character or mentor figure. This could have been a family member, an adult friend or helper. During these "moulding moments" as a child we are particularly susceptible to powerful influences of this kind. These early influences are augmented by popular media images and our own self-centred needs. Our early influences are subsequently conditioned by what we *think* about, *look* at, *receive*, *speak* and *listen* to on a daily basis.

There are higher-level desires and lower-level desires. Lower-level desires such as revenge, jealousy and bitterness are damaging to you and to others around you. Avoid lower-level desires that have a negative impact on you, on others or misuse resources. These are unworthy desires. Cleanse your motives by being accountable to others and through internal reflection. Remove resentful feelings from your heart and accept the past. Dismiss the tyranny of "should". There is no "this should be" or "that should be". There is no such thing as *should*, there only *is*! Take time out to really consider what you want to *do*, what you want to *have*, whom you want to *be* and with whom you want to *share* your life. Here are some ways to make this assessment and develop a plan of action:

- Remove mental barriers and constraints. Imagine that money and time are of no object
- Imagine what you would strive for if you knew you couldn't fail
- Construct your goals around higher level desires
- Throw out indecision and procrastination (the thieves of time and opportunity).

Setting personal goals

Goal setting is a skill and like any other skill can be acquired. There are a number of simple processes that you can establish and follow. These will enable you to plan and achieve your goals.

All goals need to be SMART. This is an acronym for Specific, Measurable, Attainable (or Achievable), Realistic and Time-bound. One crucial element in goal setting is to avoid getting bogged down in the "how to" before you have fully explored the "what" it is you truly want. You do not need to concern yourself initially with how you will achieve your goals. This comes later. Creative energies can produce an endless supply of options and potential solutions once you are fully committed to achieving clearly defined goals.

You may develop a list of dozens of goals and initially, for many of them, you may not know how they are going to be achieved. This is not a problem, provided you have been through the process of cleansing your motives to ensure that your goals are congruent with each other and with your core values.

Your core values

Decide on your core values. Develop a list of which you can take personal ownership. Here are some examples to choose from:

- truthfulness
- reliability
- justice
- consistency
- integrity
- persistency
- honesty
- approachability
- sincerity
- responsiveness
- humility
- passion
- professionalism

Categorising your goals

You may want to list your goals in categories, as follows:
- Timeframe categories
  - Short-term (e.g. immediate to six months forward)
  - Medium-term (e.g. six months to two years)
  - Long-term (e.g. two or more years forward)

Ideally, you want a combination of short, medium and long-term goals. For example, if you only have long-term goals this may not offer sufficient motivation in the present to pull you forward today.

- People-centred categories
  - ◆ Personal goals (goals you want to achieve for your own benefit)
  - ◆ Family goals (goals you want to achieve for the benefit of others in your family or circle of friends)
  - ◆ Shared goals (goals that more than one person share collective responsibility for)
  - ◆ Anonymous goals (achieving goals for the benefit of others while remaining anonymous, e.g. an anonymous charitable gift or donating a major organ for transplant)
- Resource-based categories
  - ◆ Financial cost
  - ◆ Time investment
  - ◆ Other resource requirements

All goals *must be documented* for them to have the meaningful impact you desire. Once you have your goal list in place, this then becomes a living document that can be added to and developed over time. View it regularly, daily if possible.

Pick out a few very deep-seated goals that have a high level of emotional content attributed to them. Keep these constantly in front of you by envisioning and reciting them several times a day.

Over time you can add in the "how to" achieve details for every goal. Do not be concerned about having gaps in the "how to" column. The means will become clearer as you work your way through the list. Review progress regularly, checking off completed goals and evaluating general advancement with other goals.

"Just one day of living a life with purpose is worth more than a lifetime of living without." — Brian James

The three levels of commitment

Commitment is the ability to carry out a task long after the mood in which it was created has passed. When it comes to having an overwhelming determination to achieve your goals, you are said to be truly committed. True commitment becomes a life long mission. Anything less will limit your results and water down your achievements. This can be broken down into three levels of commitment

1. I will try (most people at this level give up at the first hurdle)
2. I will give it my best (some determination for success but still not strong enough to win through all adversity)
3. It is *done* (the commitment level is so strong that you will overcome every barrier to achieve your goal).

True commitment becomes a life long mission. Anything less will limit your results and water down your achievements.

The story of a father's sacrifice

The father was becoming desperate with the deteriorating condition of his son's health. His son had an acutely damaged liver which meant that his chance of survival was very slim. His young son was dying and his father felt completely helpless. The search for a potential liver transplant had so far failed to produce a suitable donor. An appropriate match had not been found.

The father addressed the medical consultant: "Please use my liver to save my son", he pleaded. The consultant knew that the father could not survive without his own liver. He also knew that the father's liver would be a perfect match for his son. Up to now, successful liver transplants had only been conducted following the death of the donor. The consultant was aware of tests that had been undertaken on part liver transplants. They were highly risky and had been unsuccessful up to now.

Given the father's pleas and the son's acute situation the consultant agreed to take the chance. The part transfer was made. The surgery was highly successful. Six months later, both father and son were recovering to almost full health.

The father was prepared to sacrifice his own life for his son's survival. This is true commitment!

"Lifting the lid" on our capabilities

Fleas have an incredible capability of jumping 350 times their own height. This is the equivalent of a human jumping the length of a football pitch! In order to be trained for circus acts, however, fleas can be conditioned to jump only to a certain height. This is achieved by placing them in a glass flask with the lid placed on top. The fleas try to jump to their usual height but are restricted by the height of the flask. After a short time the fleas soon learn to jump just below the height of the flask so saving them the pain of hitting the lid. Subsequently, the lid is removed and the fleas continue to jump to their newly conditioned maximum height.

We are also conditioned by our previous experiences and self-limiting beliefs that are often the restricted views of others rather than our own true potential. Lift the lid off your imposed limitations. Stretch yourself to perform to your true potential.

Lift the lid off your imposed limitations. Stretch yourself to perform to your true potential.

Changing our daily habits

We are all a collection of our daily habits. We continue to operate under the same routine, often for many years, sometimes without reviewing how these habits are impacting on our lives and the achievement of our goals. Our habits are comfortable and therefore we stick with them until we choose to modify them. Some of our acquired habits are not helpful in moving us closer to the accomplishment of our dreams and aspirations. From time to time we need to review and refine our habits in order to move forward. This takes a concerted effort.

You may like to carry out the following exercise. Make a list of daily habits that you would like to modify. Make two columns, one containing supportive habits that you would like to increase and another column containing habits you would like to cut out. The following examples may help to get you started.

Habits to Make	Habits to Break
Practise active listening	Always following my own agenda
Adapting style for better communication with others	Drinking less alcohol/smoking less/ eating less etc.
Prepare and review daily to do list	Overspending or unnecessary extravagances
Daily positive reading/ physical exercise	Avoid cutting corners
Practise delayed gratification	Avoid being late for meetings
Live with passion/enjoy the moment	Taking silly risks

Modifying our daily habits

The power of positive programming

The positive beliefs we have of ourselves and others determine our behaviour and our outcomes. This can work as a *virtuous* circle to achieving our true desires. It can alternatively operate as a *vicious* circle when we constantly bombard ourselves with self-limiting beliefs.

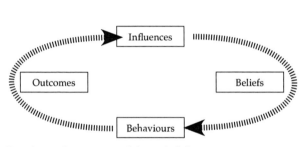

Creating a virtuous or a vicious circle?

The conscious and sub-conscious mind

In a greatly simplified way, the workings of the conscious and sub-conscious mind can be compared to parts of a computer. The conscious mind can be compared to Random Access Memory (RAM). This processes information and makes decisions based on preset criteria. Equally the sub-conscious mind can be compared to the hard drive. This stores vast amounts of data.

Conscious mind

This provides for an awareness of our world and us. This is where we rationalise and perform analysis including self-analysis (self-talk). It handles one piece of information at a time creating pictures in our mind. It is most active when we are awake, energised and alert. It is least active when we are asleep. It performs the following key functions:

- Short term memory
- Awareness
- Thinking
- Imagination
- Analysis

Sub-conscious mind

This provides for a vast store of information. To add some scale to the enormous capacity of this storage, the ratio between this and the conscious mind is estimated to be *ten million to one*. Unlike the conscious mind it does not perform any evaluation on the stored information. For example, it has no concept of time. It maintains all our vital body functions automatically and never sleeps. It performs the following multiple functions and stores information containing:

- Long-term memory
- Beliefs and values
- Self concepts
- Learned behaviour
- Our habits
- Manages all our vital functions
- Maintains our drive and energy system

Creating our reality

Our reality is formed through the combination of the conscious and sub-conscious mind working together. In long-term memory we store information based on the picture created in our mind at the time the memory was formed. The *depth and feeling* of the memory is determined by the *emotional content* that was linked to it at the time it was stored.

This means that a particularly emotional event will be stored at a deeper level within our sub-conscious mind. Upon recall we cannot differentiate between real and imagined, as everything appears real and current. We are conditioned from birth with many experiences of rejection and failure. Consequently, the majority of the content of our subconscious mind is mostly negative. This means that we can be harbouring old memories that are no longer relevant or helpful; yet to us appear equally real and valid.

Johnny's childhood memory

Johnny is a young child of seven. He is in his school classroom. He was kept behind after the others had left for home. He is sitting at his desk with his head in his hands and he is listening to what is being said. His Mother is standing behind him and his teacher is standing a short distance in front of him. His Mother is concerned about the progress he is making at school and she is having a discussion with the Teacher. Johnny is a considerate and thoughtful child of average intelligence.

His teacher responds to his Mother's concerns and says, "Unfortunately, Johnny appears to be struggling with spelling and arithmetic. He is not particularly bright so probably will never amount to much". His teacher does not realise the *deep level of psychological damage* done to Johnny that day as he carries that view of himself into adult life.

A self-fulfilling prophecy

Our self-image determines our performance. Our self-image is made up of the combined experiences and memories we have stored in our sub-conscious. This is constantly reinforced through our self-talk. When we have a positive view of ourselves this creates positive results. Conversely when we think negatively this produces negative results. Because of the huge size of our sub-conscious store of information, it will always win over conflicts with the conscious mind.

Our self-image determines our performance.

Repairing the damage that results from many years of negative input cannot be reversed instantaneously. It requires concerted effort over a period of time. We can deliberately construct conflicts into our conscious mind to begin the process of introducing some new positive thoughts that we want to become "good" habits. Constant repetition and reinforcement of positive input over time will produce the desired behaviours and subsequent outcomes.

Our drive and energy systems work together and are fuelled by being passionate about our goals and objectives. Sub-conscious negatives and negative input from others also drain our drive and energy systems. This can be counteracted with positive reprogramming statements

(PRS) or affirmations. In addition our energy levels are raised with a good diet and regular exercise. Combined together this provides the energies required to sustain a *programme that can transform your life.*

Turning negative into positive

This is an exercise that you can undertake to support your efforts to positively reprogram your subconscious mind. This is a three-stage process. Start by listing out the most damaging and limiting negative beliefs that you have acquired about yourself. Taking your top ten is a reasonable number to work with. Concentrate on the negative beliefs that you feel most hold you back from the success you desire.

Secondly, reword the list taking each negative statement and turning it into a positive statement. Lastly, read out the positive statements on a regular basis, daily ideally. Within 30 days you will start to notice a significant difference in your self-esteem.

Here are some examples in the table below. They may or may not apply to you. Use and adapt them to your own circumstances:

Negative Statement	Reworded Positive Statement
I am not clever enough to achieve the things I want in my life	I am clever enough to succeed to the extent that I am prepared to work and grow. I have bright intelligence and an alert mental capacity
I find exams difficult and often fail to reach the required standard	I pass the exams required to reach my chosen goals. I enjoy study and learning to earn the qualifications I need to succeed

Negative Statement	Reworded Positive Statement
I find it difficult to communicate effectively with some types of people	I get on well with everybody I meet. I work through challenges to communicate effectively at every level and with every person
I take longer to achieve success in new areas compared to others and can be slow to reach competence	I work hard and fast to achieve my goals quickly and efficiently. I achieve my objectives within the deadlines I set
I sometimes lack confidence in my abilities	I am very self confident and am capable of anything that I choose to work for according to the priorities I set myself
I make mistakes when under pressure to perform	I learn from past mistakes and do not repeat them even under pressure. Experience is a great teacher
I feel threatened in public places when faced with many strangers	I am able to be confident and self assured in any public place and with any other people present
I lack natural talents such as ... e.g. social, musical, language abilities etc.	I have numerous natural talents and resources that I maximise to achieve my goals, winning through setbacks and adversity
My (height, weight, shape etc.) acts as a disadvantage while around other people who are (taller, shorter, thinner, broader)	I stand erect and upright with excellent posture and am not intimidated by others who are (taller, shorter, thinner, broader)
I have a poor memory for names, people, places and past events	I am great at remembering names, people, places and important events. My sub-conscious mind works in harmony with my conscious mind to recall the information I need when I need it.

Turning negative into positive

David's heroic rescue

David and his younger brother Jim were delighted to see that it had snowed overnight. The new day was cold, clear and dry. David turned excitedly to Jim and said, "We can go ice skating on the lake."

They hurriedly rushed downstairs and gulped down their breakfast. With a quick hug from their Mum and a promise to be careful, they were soon off out into the fresh air and making their way.

After a short walk across the crisp newly laid snow they entered the forest. A little further on and they had reached their destination. There was a clearing in the forest and before them stretched a large lake with the frozen surface glinting like a million diamonds reflecting the morning sunlight. David and Jim quickly unpacked their bags and replaced their boots with ice skates.

They were both exhilarated by the cool light breeze in their faces as they skated up, down and around near the edge of the lake. Suddenly without warning David heard a splintering sound and a cry from his younger brother as the thin ice he had skated over gave way to the weight. David turned to discover what had happened. In an instant, Jim had fallen into the cold dark water below and the broken block of ice had resurfaced into its previous position leaving no sign of young Jim.

Immediately David reacted. He skated without fear of his own life towards the area where Jim had vanished. He looked around him. What could he do to save his brother? He had nothing to help him. No rope to use. He just had his bare hands under the warm gloves. He thought quickly. His mind was racing. What could he do?

At that moment he caught the glimpse of an old tree overhanging the edge of the lake some distance away. He was a fast skater and sped to the edge. He broke off a large branch and dragged it back to the gruesome spot where his brother had sunk into the abyss below. He pounded the surface of the ice with the branch without effect at first.

Harder and harder he thumped the ice with the branch. Five times, ten times, fifteen times and more.

Eventually he heard a cracking noise as the ice slowly yielded to the pounding. Still he battered away until he finally broke the surface and a gap appeared in the ice. A little distance away he caught a glimpse of his brother's red jacket bobbing just beneath the surface. He used the branch to pull Jim to the edge. A few more seconds and he was by his side pulling him from the freezing water back on to the frozen surface. Jim gulped and spluttered and began to come round. He was alive! He was going to survive.

The noise had attracted attention from others nearby, walking their dogs or having a brisk early morning jog. Before long a crowd had gathered to watch the scene unfolding. The ambulance came and collected Jim and his heroic brother. They were soon on their way to the nearest hospital to complete Jim's recovery.

The group of onlookers observed the scene in amazement. They could see the shattered ice next to the large branch, the still chilled water gently lapping against the sharp edges of the broken ice and the tree in the distance. One of them broke the silence. "This is unbelievable." He challenged. "That branch must be many feet long and several inches thick. How could a boy tear it from that tree and pull it all that distance? And even then, how could he have lifted it to break the ice and rescue his brother? It must weigh a ton." The onlookers gasped with incredulity as they all began to realise the enormity of the task that the boy had achieved.

An elderly gentleman had been having a stroll by the lake and had stopped with the others who had now gathered. He stepped forward. He began to speak with dignity and passion and said, "I know exactly how the boy did it". The others turned to listen to the words of wisdom as he continued. "It is simply that no one was here to tell him it could not be done!"

How we feed our minds

How we feed our minds determines the kind of person we become. If you want to become more fulfilled by working on and achieving your goals you need to be sensitive to how you feed your mind. Small minded people tend to focus on the acts of others that they disagree with. That is often their chosen topic of conversation. If you are looking to expand your mind then avoid the practice of complaining, criticising and condemning others. Great people focus on ideas, concepts and events to help them and others achieve their goals. You can achieve all you want in life if you help enough other people get what they want.

Great people focus on ideas,
concepts and events to help them
and others achieve their goals.

Keeping an ideas file can help you to capture and exploit the best options and possible solutions to overcoming challenges. Keep a pad with you at all times to record the idea as soon as it comes into your mind. *Missed ideas can be lost forever if not immediately recorded.* Review your ideas file from time to time. Retain ideas while they still appear to have merit. Discard those that are unworkable. Over time you will establish a Pandora's Box full of gems that will inspire you to maximise your creative thinking possibilities.

When times get really tough

We all go through cycles of difficult times. When times are tough the tough keep moving and working through their challenges. *Tough times will not last forever.* At some stage you will break out of the negative cycle and your life will begin to blossom again. However bad these difficult times become, *these times too will pass.*

You may have suffered from extreme financial pressures. You may have suffered a bereavement of a family member or close friend. You may have had severe health problems. However bad it has been or becomes, *you can handle it with inner strength*. The following truths may help you at extreme times of crisis.

- As long as you keep breathing you can keep living
- You always have the capacity to love yourself and others
- Apart from impulse situations you are always in control of how you respond to situations and circumstances
- You can always learn more, gaining greater knowledge, insight and wisdom
- You can always have faith in your ability and the ability of others
- You can create and leave a legacy for others
- You can have purpose to your life

Becoming great

The following is a list of positive statements towards becoming great. You may choose to use some of them for your own personal development. As you build your own list, construct statements that describe your goals as already achieved or well on the way towards completion.

- My business is growing like crazy and everyone I talk to is becoming a client
- My business is easy. My business is exploding
- I have no money worries. Money flows to me easily and naturally
- I am a winner moving forward and giving to others
- I am leading myself and others to a better life
- I am becoming the best I can be, the hero/heroine of my family, a highly inspirational public speaker, an accomplished author and a successful entrepreneur
- I am becoming a great leader of great leaders
- I enjoy my business and working with my people
- I am the most positive, enthusiastic, committed, influential and confident person I know
- I am designed to be the person I dream of becoming

- I will soar like an eagle and reach any level of success I choose
- I choose to be free. I constantly strive for my freedom
- I am winning my independence. I am unstoppable.

Be committed. Keep your goals in front of you and keep moving forward as you succeed.

Final thoughts

Be committed. Keep your goals in front of you and keep moving forward as you succeed. Remember, a big shot is a little shot who just kept shooting.

Interview with
Simon Woodroffe

What does success mean to Simon Woodroffe?
Success for me is not having no money, it is that simple. I went through a lot of my life feeling financially insecure. I am not saying that I was poor most of my life because I wasn't but I was on the verge of it. So not being poor is success and anything above that is the cream for me.

Have you always been an entrepreneur?
I left school when I was sixteen and after a couple of years you do look around you and think, nobody else is going to do it for me. I have no qualifications to fall back on, so in that sense, yes I have always been an entrepreneur because I have always had to think on my feet, think how I can earn a living and think how I can do things. I remember quite early on when I was a student at Cambridge, not the university but Cambridge Tech, which I wasn't at for very long and I did not get any qualifications. It was in the hippy times of the sixties and I remember starting to make snakeskin belts and going up to the leather place where you buy the snakeskin and realising the difference between wholesale and retail. It was a simple realisation. I thought, this is good, in that you could buy something very cheap, put it together and sell it for a lot more. I was always turned on by that as a way of earning a living.

How did the YO! Sushi story begin?
Well , it is a famous story now, the YO! Sushi story, but I was coming up to forty and I had been a designer of big rock shows and I had been in the television business and people said to me well, 'you are successful'. But inside I felt that I had under achieved and not yet fulfilled my potential. And I started looking at lots of different things that I was going to do, just doing the research because if you are anything like me and you have an idea, on the Monday

you are going to do it, on the Tuesday you are not going to do it and on the Wednesday you have changed your mind again. It is on off, on off. So I ban myself from making a decision as to whether I am going to do something or not and then ultimately the decision tends to make itself.

So I was coming up to forty and I was sitting in a restaurant with a guy I knew from the TV business. I was saying what about this and what about that and what about sushi, because I think in the back of my mind I was thinking I could produce a factory. It was really a bit of a throwaway and he looked at me and he said, 'what you should do Simon is a conveyer belt sushi bar with girls in black PVC miniskirts' as that was his kind of style thing and I remember thinking in that moment that maybe that is what I am going to do. So I went away and researched it and two years later I opened the first YO! Sushi and it was a success.

How tough was it to make the business happen?
When I look back at that two years when I got YO! Sushi together, I almost do not recognise the person because I think to myself, 'how did I do that?' That is unbelievable that I did that and I think it was through enormous hard work and persistence. People say to me, 'what did you do during those two years?' and I say it was very, very hard work; it was a very tough time.

There were two things that I did not have. I knew that I could get the restaurant together. I could get the restaurant designed, I could get the operators. I believed I could do all that but I did not have any money. I had £150,000 tied up in my home which I decided to put into the business, but I did not want to start a £150,000 restaurant business. I wanted to start something that was a big deal right at the end of the nineties but I did not have any track record in the restaurant business. So the other problem was to find a landlord who would let me have a big deal site. So those were the two hardest things to do.

In terms of getting support, I am a great listener and I will always listen to people even if they have the C word at the front, the Consultant word. I will always listen, but I will never take advice and there is a difference. In the end the decision of the entrepreneur for me has to be with them. After all why would anyone else know? People say to me, 'do you think I should do it?' and I say, 'well only you know that' as only I know that for me I am a great one for researching and for listening but there is a firewall. I do not make decisions based on the market research—I educate myself with market research but I make decisions based on instinct as to whether I think it is right.

How did you raise the money?

I had that £150,000 from the house and I had a childhood friend called Matthew Gibb and a friend of his (who I met on a street in Paris actually) and between them they put up £50,000. So I suppose you could say that was a belief in that Matthew backed me. He knew me. I often say that a great place to get money is from friends and family. Usually in start-up situations, the people who are going to give you the money is somebody you already know and people send out all these letters all over the place and business plans when actually you already know the person. A lot of the time that is wasted energy in my view. So, that was where the first money came from and I found a bank manager who was sympathetic and I took him along to the first YO! Sushi bar in Liverpool Street in London that was doing very well and he said he would put himself behind it and I got a government loan scheme of £100,000 and that was all. I never had any equity to put in. Therefore I had £350,000 but I needed £700,000 as I had already pressed the button because I thought I was going to get the rest via private equity. But they never did, well they did eventually but by the time we opened I had already pressed the button without everything being in place. By the time we opened, those guys were ready with their cheque books and eventually I got extended credit from one of my suppliers. I later asked them why they gave me extended credit and they said, 'because you had those big Japanese sponsors behind you, Sony and Honda'. The truth was they had given me peanuts. Sony had lent me some TVs and I just used the Honda name. He said he gave me extended credit because I had all those big Japanese companies behind me and they would never let me go down!

Was that Japanese connection a ploy you had planned?

Not really, I just did it instinctively. I went out and got some sponsors because I thought I could get the TVs cheap and, when it came to it, that is what happened. Very often I find that life is, as John Lennon says, what happens when you are busy making other plans

What is your advice to would-be entrepreneurs?

Well first of all, I think that making a million pounds is not that difficult at all. I think making five million pounds is difficult, but making one million pounds isn't that difficult. I think anyone has the potential capability of doing it. I think you have to be desperate though. You have to just sacrifice everything, literally, I would say and be prepared to do whatever it takes and become obsessed with getting it done. If you have the aspiration, you need to put yourself on the line. I don't think as human beings we do really difficult things out of the desire for great pleasure, we tend to do it through the fear of great pain. If you are in a war you do not go and kill off a machine gun nest because you might get the medal at the end, you do it because if you don't, the whole thing might fall apart and you feel the weight of responsibility. So one of the things I would say to people is do the research first. Don't decide whether you are going to do it at the beginning. People sit around and think, 'I have got this great idea but I dont know whether I should do it or shouldnt do it' and actually you can never make the decision just based on that point at the beginning. You have to do the research. Put some time and some money in and be absolutely willing to lose that time and money to do the research. Maybe have two or three things on the go and then, when you get to that point, usually the decision will tend to make itself and then you are on the treadmill to getting to it. Sometimes people give up but if it has got substance to it and you have done the research at the beginning, you have a chance of getting it but it is not painless, that is for sure!

Do people really appreciate how hard it is to start a business?

I think that you really have to want to do it. That two years was hard work but they were also very halcyon years. I remember at the time thinking, 'this is the best fun'. I had my 150 grand, I wasn't living off much money thinking, 'should I break into this fiver?'. I never went to dinner. A mean sod! But it was a very enjoyable period because I thought I had something, I truly believed I had something. I wasn't being judged, I didn't have to look at the figures on Monday morning to see if it was working or not. Everybody was saying, 'what a great idea' and so it was very enjoyable in those days.

Do people know what they are going to go through?

I think that if you really knew what you were going to go through in this life, I think we all have a bit of denial which is probably pretty healthy, because if you really knew what you are going to go through you would not do it. If Kriss Akabusi for example had thought about all the pain he was going to go through he wouldn't have done what he did.

What is next for the YO! brand and Simon Woodroffe?

I sold the controlling interest in YO! Sushi in the summer and that had always been my aim. In fact I probably should have done it a few years before. So that was a very good feeling because I thought, 'right, done that, got a result from it, got some cash in the bank and I am still involved and have a substantial interest in the company which will give me a good financial return at some point'.

I have always stepped up and said that what I am trying to do is become the next Virgin, 'YO! Everything Else' we call it and I have never really felt free to go out and do that until we got YO! Sushi away. I have licensed 'YO! Japan' as a clothing range to a company and their passion is to make YO! Japan a major clothing thing, so that's one we have done. 'YO!tel' is the next one and then I have got in development with a guy called Rob Gregory a spa called 'YO!zone' so there are a few things. That is three businesses I am doing with YO!.

I do a lot of public speaking. I want to present more television. I think that this entrepreneurs' society thing is great and TV is the way to make it all happen. I think that the new cooking on TV will be entrepreneurs and I think that this website and your planned TV channel is exactly what that is about and spot on for this moment in time. I think that the business people will be the new heroes and pop stars and film stars. I certainly hope so!

Do we have a true enterprise culture in the UK?

First of all, I think that Gordon Brown is absolutely right. I know Gordon and we have talked about it and he is absolutely right in that we were a nation of shopkeepers— my words not his—and I think we will be a nation of entrepreneurs. I think that we are a very creative nation, a bold nation, we have been explorers all our life. I think we have great taste and hold that velvet purse in terms of taste in design and I think to have a nation of entrepreneurs is exactly the right business strategy for this country. So I think Gordon Brown is right. I am certainly behind making that happen. I don't think it is something that governments make happen, I think it is something that grows over time. I think television is absolutely what it is about.

Cooking and food in this country did not change through theories or governments, it happened through television and that has been the inspiration for a nation to start eating out. If you think of the change that has happened over the last ten years with food, that same change can happen for business. It goes deeper than that actually, I think that what I call the acceptable face of personal development, which was an embarrassing word ten years ago, is what is happening in big corporations now. I had our bank manager round the other day and he said that on Monday mornings they all get together and sit round in a circle and share. That is a bank! Unbelievable! So what I hear big corporations talking about now is finding creativity in their businesses, finding entrepreneurial spirits within their businesses and bringing people on. This whole focus is on people and that is effectively what entrepreneurs do, they are actually willing to confront the limiting things that hold them back from going out and succeeding. Whether it is the fear of success, the fear of failure or whatever it is—usually something to do with fear—when confidence happens to large numbers of people over a nation, unbelievable things could happen on that level. It is only twenty years ago, fifteen years ago even, that if you sat in the factory toilet reading the *Sun* newspaper all your colleagues would be saying, 'Yes! Beat the management'! We were a skiving culture, that is what we come from, but now I see the beginnings of people celebrating success and applauding it rather than cynically saying, 'ah he can do it, I can't'.

How do you create a work life balance?

What I talk about in relation to work life balance is how I live my life. People call me up now and they say, we know you are really busy but I won't take a minute of your time, and I go,' I am not' and I think that this busy thing is a state of mind. I don't want to be completely, obsessively busy. I don't function well under that sort of stress. What I do is, despite all the projects I have set up, I do not run any of them now. They are all run by other people and I am perhaps the seed financier or perhaps I am a mentor and certainly I have creative idea as to how things should be done, so the ideas come from me but I ask other people do it, so effectively I don't have people working for me as such. I have a PA and that is about it. At some level those other people are partners.

In my life, on the one hand and I say, 'on the one shoulder', I am extremely serious about what I do. I am absolutely committed. I want to work with the very best people to do the very best things and that is on this left shoulder and on the right shoulder though, I really do not give a damn because in the light of the world and life and love and your children and we are all going to die and everything, you know YO! Sushi and YO! Everything Else is not very important, I can tell you.

What books have inspired and helped you along the way?

The book that inspired me when I was a very young man, was *Seven Years in Tibet*. It was a much better book than it was a film about this adventurer, a German actually, who went to Tibet and met the Dalai Lama and all that spiritual adventure stuff. Then, over the years, I read all the personal development books all the how to be a millionaire books, well actually when I say I read them, I read the first chapter of most of them and I skipped through the rest because I haven't got the concentration to focus on all of it. So in truth, I am not a great reader, in a sense.

Then there were people like Julian Richer who wrote *The Richer Way* who talks about customer service. In business I do not use buzz words. You hear some of these consultants and management gurus talking and they make it sound so complicated when, actually, to open a shop and sell something is about great customer service, buying for less and selling for more. They can be pretty simple businesses really and I think Julian Richer is someone who wrote about the nitty gritty or what it takes to do something and pay attention to detail and that is what he calls ATD, Attention to Detail.

How would you like to be remembered?

Well, it is a funny thing but I am not really old enough to have got to that stage where I look back over my life yet, but one of the things I have aspired to do is look back and say, 'wasn't that great when I did this or did that'. Certainly I am proud of what I did and I am proud of YO! Sushi. I am very, very proud of that and it was a very tough thing to do.

I think for me it is about becoming the person you want to be. To be on your death bed and say I have actually changed enough, because people say I cannot change, this is who I am but the thing that I have learned is that you can change anything about yourself. Your habits, how you have been brought up, your limiting beliefs, you can change all that stuff. It is absolutely changeable if you come out of the denial of it and just face up to it. That is it for me, seeing my arrogant side, my controlling side, seeing the fear I have around money. Seeing all of those things, because once you see them the power comes to you. So I hope one day I will look back and say, 'I became the person that I wanted to be', but I am not there yet.

IIIIIIIIIIIIIIIIIIIIIIIIIIIIIIIIIIIIIIIIIIIIIIIIIIIIIIIIIIIIIIIIIIIIIIIII

Simon Woodroffe founded YO! Sushi in 1997 followed by a host of spin-offs including YO! Below and YO! to Go with which he hopes to eclipse Virgin and Easy.

In 2003 he sold a controlling stake to the management team. YO! Japan clothing launched in 2003 and it is now sold in 300 outlets in 12 countries. YOTEL is set to open in 2007 and a spa concept is in development.

The first screening in early 2005 of BBC's *Dragons' Den* established Simon as a successful TV personality. Simon believes that business will be the source for the next wave of reality based TV and is working on a number of television concepts based around this.

IIIIIIIIIIIIIIIIIIIIIIIIIIIIIIIIIIIIIIIIIIIIIIIIIIIIIIIIIIIIIIIIIIIIIIIII

Watch this video interview plus many more like it through your free subscription to online business TV portal Expertsonline.tv available to you as a buyer of this book. Just send an e-mail to **info@expertsonline.tv**, *including*

the ISBN number, and the location of where you bought the book to receive your free subscription worth £50.

Chapter 3

Business planning

"Destiny is not a matter of chance. It is a matter of choice. It is not a thing to be waited for. It is a thing to be achieved."—William Jennings Bryan

By failing to plan, you are in effect planning to fail. By preparing a written plan, you can avoid many of the pitfalls that plague businesses the world over. Your plan will provide the guidance you need to steer the appropriate course. Your plan can take full account of risk factors such as competitive forces and changing market conditions. How beneficial would it be for you and your business, if you were able to minimise these risks? This is achievable through a well-constructed plan that is flexible and meets the demanding needs of your business.

Why have strategic plans?
We plan because we want our business or organisation to be successful. We want to take advantage of timely opportunity to drive our business forward. We want a clear understanding of where our business is and where it is going. One of the main benefits of sound planning is that you gain clarity of purpose and a laser-like focus to the fulfilment of your goals and objectives. This provides clear action steps required to achieve the goals. Following the steps will create results. Refining the steps will lead to success.

---

*One of the main benefits of
sound planning is that you gain
clarity of purpose and a laser-like
focus to the fulfilment of your
goals and objectives.*

The progress of your business moves from birth to infancy to adolescence to maturity. This is like going on a journey where your business is the vehicle and you don't want to crash! Any journey begins with the destination in mind. Your strategic plan is the map of the journey. To continue with this analogy consider a major journey in a car. Would you do the following?

- Leave without knowing where you are going
- Get in without knowing how to get out
- Begin without having a clear idea of the route and a map
- Not knowing how to refuel along the way
- Ignorant of what to do if your car has a breakdown
- Unaware of how many passengers are taking the journey with you
- Unclear as to who is driving

Business failure is often associated with the poor handling of major risks. Most new businesses fail in the first five years and these are some of the key reasons:

- Unwillingness to adapt to market changes
- Lack of essential market knowledge
- Lack of taking appropriate advice
- Poor financial management leading to insolvency
- Not able to provide consistent results for customers

A good structured plan that is followed enables these issues to be managed.

What will strategic planning deliver?

A workable strategic plan does not have to be a mammoth sized document that fills up space in your bookcase without ever being used. For the plan to be a worthwhile business tool it needs to be a document that reflects your vision and strategic goals. Your plan needs to be a dynamic contract between owners, staff, suppliers and channel partners. It needs to provide a blueprint towards establishing, communicating and fulfilling your business objectives. A good plan will clearly show you the circumstances and reasons behind your progress. A good plan will provide answers to the following questions:

- Where is your business now?
- How did you arrive here?
- Where are you headed if you continue on your current path?
- Where do you really want to be?
- When do you want to arrive at your chosen destination?
- What's the fastest route to getting there?

Your plan needs to be a dynamic contract between owners, staff, suppliers and channel partners.

The Main elements of a strategic plan
The main elements of a workable strategic plan include:

- Recent history of key business financial factors
- Clear goals for the future
- Implementation of goals using financial, time-based and people resources
- Documented action steps
- Follow up process

Typical goals for business owners include financial independence, having control and being fulfilled. The main barriers to achieving these goals are overwork, stress, cash flow constraints and unreasonable customer demands. The main elements of a plan can be broken down further into a number of essential requirements:

1. SMART (Specific, Measurable, Achievable, Realistic and Timed) objectives for profitability together with a review process
2. An exit strategy
3. Means of producing consistent results for customers
4. Details of sales and marketing activities applied to your market
5. Business functions manageable in house and those required to be outsourced
6. Clear organisational structure now and in the future
7. Resource requirements of time, money, people and premises
8. Management of customer and staff expectations
9. Effective compliance to manage legal and ethical risks

In order to put your plan into practice there needs to be a willingness to be adaptable. You require the availability of reliable advice. You need an ongoing means of applying effective sales and marketing effort with a refinement process in place. You need to manage key risks namely financial, legal and moral. You require ongoing development of skills and knowledge.

The following is a step-by-step guide with examples to preparing a simple strategic plan, split into three sections. You can use this to develop your own plan. Please note this is intended as a guide to assist you in your own strategic planning and is not designed for capital raising purposes from external sources.

Financial considerations

For existing businesses, list your turnover, sales costs, gross margin, fixed costs and net profit before tax (NPBT) for last year. Then repeat this for previous years. If possible it is useful to go back three to five years for trend analysis purposes.

Year (past)	3	2	1
Turnover	£1,272,000	£1,600,000	£2,000,000
Sales Costs	£737,000	£950,000	£1,100,000
Gross Margin	£535,000	£650,000	£900,000
Fixed Costs	£373,000	£400,000	£550,000
NPBT*	£162,000	£250,000	£350,000
Profit %	12.74%	15.62%	17.50%

Net profit before tax
Historic financial data

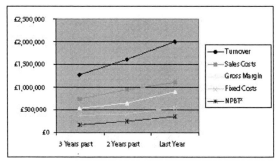

Past 3-Years Historical

It is important to separate sales costs from fixed (or general operating) costs. *Sales costs represent the direct hard costs of producing sales.* This includes, for example, the cost of an advertisement, a sales campaign, the cost of raw materials and sales related bonuses or commissions. You are therefore able to establish the gross profitability of your collective sales and marketing activities.

Separately, you also want to be aware of the gross profitability of each sales and marketing activity individually. For example, in year 3 above the average gross margin is approximately 42% (£535,000/£1,272,000*100). This may be made up of various activities, some much more profitable than others. You are therefore able to identify these activities for refinement purposes, to make them more profitable or to stop doing them if they are not capable of contributing to profit. *As you grow your turnover, you need to know what costs are going to increase proportionately with sales.* Your gross margin calculation must therefore accurately reflect this. Different accounting disciplines means that your management accounts may not automatically provide this information for you, so you may need to have it calculated separately for business planning purposes.

Fixed (or operating) costs, on the other hand, are your general overhead costs. This includes staff salaries (excluding sales related bonuses), organisational costs and expenses. *Fixed costs do not rise proportionately with increases in sales but rather they increase in bands as your organisation grows.* For example, the difference in fixed costs in year 3 above (£373,000), compared to year 1 (£550,000) reflects a greater number of staff and larger premises that are required to produce the higher turnover levels.

In order for your business to sustain itself the net profit before tax (NPBT) needs to exceed the cost of raising capital. This way your business can always support a requirement for raising capital to manage any cash flow constraints.

Defining your exit strategy

Define what it is you want from your business. Your personal goal list (from Chapter 2) will assist you in this process. Do you want to sell the business, pass it on to another family member or launch the business as a public company? In order to plan effectively, you need to decide on the following:

- Date of exit
- Required turnover and profitability levels
- Individual Shareholder and overall capital value of the business
- Preferred exit route

*Define what it is you want from
your business.*

Potential exit routes

Your route to exit will depend upon several factors. Many of the factors may not become apparent until you are actually ready to carry out your exit strategy. It is worth considering, however some of the key options and considerations as part of the planning process. How you structure your business or organisation will have an impact on the options available to you.

The main options for exit include:
- Trade sale (an outright sale to a third party)
- Merger (a part sale by combining with another business and continuing to trade)
- Management buy out (MBO. The sale of the business to the existing management team)
- Management buy in (MBI. The sale of the business to an external management team. Can be combined with a management buy out: BIMBO)
- Flotation (raising capital by obtaining a listing on the stock exchange and offering shares to the public)

Exit options: advantages and disadvantages

The table below provides an outline of the key implications for managing alternative exit routes. This is a complex area requiring specific professional advice at the time of exit. It is important to consider human resource and taxation implications.

Option	Advantages	Disadvantages
Trade sale	Enables you to walk away from the business and retire. May attract Venture Capital (VC)	You may receive less value than you expect. New owner may discard existing staff
Merger	You may be able to continue some involvement and management input	Matching different cultures and values often proves challenging
Management buy out	Key human resources are retained. Less unsettling for existing staff. Perceived as lower risk by VCs	Not all of the Management team may wish take part and some may struggle to find required capital
Management buy in	Fresh injection of ideas and human resource	Significant and disruptive change management issues
Flotation	Ability to raise substantial capital whilst continuing to have involvement yourself	Very costly. Reduced or Loss of control

Pros and cons of various exit routes

Your existing customer profile

Taking stock of your existing customer profile is a key part of your effective planning strategy. Assessing the lifetime value of your existing customer base is essential to this.

Most marketing activity tends to be focused on immediate profit. Focus on profit is essential for the ongoing well being of any business. Immediate profit needs in isolation, however, ignores the true value to your business of an ongoing satisfied and loyal customer base.

---

*You will receive a substantial
boost to your business when
you recognise and market to the
"lifetime value" of your customers.*

You will receive a substantial boost to your business when you recognise and market to the "lifetime value" of your customers. This assuming, of course, that you are in business long term and you are looking to develop ongoing repeat orders from worthwhile customers. Your existing customer base is your most valuable business asset. Even for businesses with one-off purchases, it is possible to create ongoing repeat business from loyal customers. This is explained more fully in later chapters.

What is "lifetime value"?

Lifetime value is the accumulated value of your customers to your business, over the duration of the customer relationship. For example, we will assume that your average customer produces £100 of profit per year and you keep them on average for 5 years. Then lifetime value of each customer is on average £500.

Once this is realised, this can become a revelation and can be instrumental in driving your business forward substantially.

With each marketing activity, by being aware of this factor and marketing to lifetime value instead of immediate profit, your business will take on a completely different shape. You will be prepared to invest appropriately to maximise responses.

Marketing using "lifetime value"

Let's compare immediate profit with lifetime value:

Over 1 Year	Immediate Profit	Lifetime Value
Investment per customer	5	50

Over 1 Year	Immediate Profit	Lifetime Value
Number of marketing activities	2	20
Sales value	100	1,000
Gross Profit	10	100

Recognising lifetime value

The table assumes that each customer produces 10% gross profit and 50% of the marketing activities produce extra sales. *This produces ten times more profitability per year per customer—wow!*

Planning for growth

You can make forward projections based on your plans for growth. At the highest level this includes the same turnover and profit figures used to assess your past and current position, but instead projected forward. The table below shows examples:

Year (forward)	1	2	3
Turnover	£3,000,000	£5,000,000	£10,000,000
Sales Costs	£1,800,000	£2,500,000	£4,800,000
Gross Margin	£1,200,000	£2,500,000	£5,200,000
Fixed Costs	£600,000	£750,000	£1,100,000
NPBT*	£600,000	£1,750,000	4,100,000
Profit %	20%	35%	41%

Net profit before tax
Financial projections

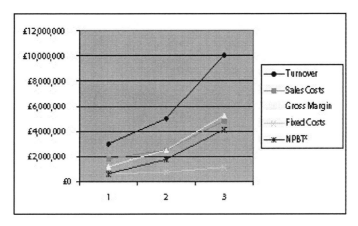

Next 3-Year Projections

As the turnover increases with greater sales volumes you may be able to benefit from improved economies of scale. For example, you may be able to negotiate better discounts from suppliers due to larger volumes of merchandise being purchased. If you are in a service industry and are not able to improve supplier deals, you may be able to cap some of your sales costs and still benefit from economies of scale. Your advertising budget, for example, could be capped. *As your turnover grows therefore, your sales costs may not have to rise in proportion to the increase in turnover.* In the examples given in the table above, sales costs reduce from 60% of turnover in year 1 (£1,800/£3,000,000) to 48% in year 3 (£4,800,000/£10,000,000). Be sure to factor these elements into your planning process.

You will also need to consider your cash flow needs as your business expands. Functions such as credit control become far more critical and need to be managed effectively.

Case Study

A specialist IT outsourcing organisation with a great message not reflected in their website nor communicated effectively to existing customers and partners because their existing technology did not allow non-technical people to manage and change it. They also wanted to set up an internal employee information exchange that was easy to maintain. By using leading edge Internet based tools they were provided with a totally integrated system to address the management of the new website, customer and partner extranets and the employee portal. This enabled them to win several new valuable customer contracts whilst managing their resources more effectively.

Your marketing methods

List all of your current sales and marketing methods and how they contribute to profitable turnover. Taking the previous example from the table headed "Historic financial data"; you can consider the gross margin for each element of marketing activity. Ignore any fixed costs in your calculations. For example, do not include premises costs or non-sales related staff costs.

Marketing method	Element	Turnover produced	Sales Costs	Gross margin
Personal selling	Field sales	£1,000,000	£670,000	£330,000
Personal selling	Trade shows	£100,000	£80,000	£20,000
Direct marketing	Telemarketing	£350,000	£160,000	£190,000
Direct marketing	Direct mail	£250,000	£60,000	£190,000
Advertising	Local press	£20,000	£15,000	£5,000
Advertising	Yellow pages	£30,000	£20,000	£10,000
Sales promotions	Manufacturer incentives	£200,000	£75,000	£125,000
Public relations	Press releases	£50,000	£20,000	£30,000

Marketing method	Element	Turnover produced	Sales Costs	Gross margin
	Total	£2,000,000	£1,100,000	£900,000

Gross margin produced from each element of marketing activity

You can now undertake analysis to determine what activity is producing most gross profit. From the table above, the combination of Field sales, telemarketing, direct mail and manufacturer incentives amounts to £835,000 in gross margin. This equates to almost 93% of the total gross margin of £900,000.

It makes most sense to refine the activities that are producing the greatest share of the gross margin before spending time developing less profitable activities.

It makes most sense to refine the activities that are producing the greatest share of the gross margin before spending time developing less profitable activities. If the effectiveness of those four activities could be improved by say 10% over a three-month period, then this would produce over £83,000 increase in bottom line profitability. For activities that you believe are not able to be refined to produce worthwhile gross profit, you may want to cut them out altogether.

Time spent performing key business functions

You may also like to review the time spent performing key business functions. You would want to include Sales, Marketing, Operations, Human resource management and Research and development, plus any other key business functions that are being performed. By reviewing total man-hours spent in each of these activities, you may be able to increase overall productivity substantially.

People Resource considerations

Complete an organisational structure diagram for your current staffing levels. The following is an example of a typical business structure.

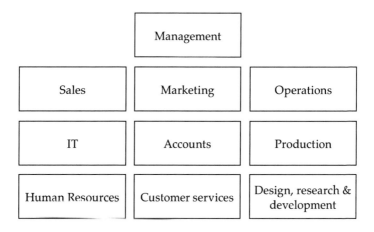

Typical organisational structure

Taking your current staffing levels you can link people to various functions within your organisation. In some cases you may have shared responsibilities across functions. *You may also want to review roles and responsibilities to match skills with appropriate roles.* Some of your key functions may be outsourced to various external suppliers and advisers.

It is essential to have a clear appreciation of how your existing people resources are managing the various functions within your organisation. You are then able to establish the likely resource requirements that will be needed to support your planned business objectives in say one, three and five years' time.

*It is important to understand
to what extent your people
are working to their strengths
and are equipped to perform
effectively in their role.*

Roles and responsibilities

The following is a questionnaire that can be used to review roles and responsibilities. It is important to understand to what extent your people are working to their strengths and are equipped to perform effectively in their role. The questionnaire can help you ascertain this information. It can be completed by all staff or alternatively by managers and supervisors only.

1. List the main duties carried out as part of your role.
2. State the proportion of your working day that relates to each of these duties. (Use percentages.)
3. How would you change these proportions to increase the effectiveness of your working day?
4. What core skills do you use in carrying out your role (e.g. Management, communication, listening, organisational, secretarial etc.)?
5. What suggestions do you have to enable more time to be spent working more effectively?
6. How do you see your role developing in future (e.g. changes to regular activities, extra responsibilities etc.)?
7. What personal skills would you like to develop in order to work more effectively?
8. What is your view of the level of customer satisfaction within your area of the business (if appropriate, this can include both external and internal customers i.e. other staff members as well as outside customers)?
9. What suggestions do you have for increasing customer satisfaction (both internal and external)?

10. State any other suggestions you have for improving the overall efficiency of the business.

Your strategic plan

Having considered your key business objectives and matched these against your current and required future resource needs you are then able to map out a list of action steps to move you forward. These are the steps needed to take you to the successful completion of your business goals.

You may find it useful to list two distinct columns of activities. One column containing activities that you wish to increase and the other containing activities you wish to reduce or eliminate. *Make sure you include a review process and allocate responsibilities to individuals for completion of each activity.* The following table lists examples of how this could operate:

Activities to start or increase	Activities to reduce or eliminate	Priority	Timescale	Who
Produce cash flow forecast to meet growth plan		High	2 weeks. Review quarterly	
Produce a detailed Marketing plan		High	1 month then annually	
Calculate and monitor customer lifetime value		High	1 week then ongoing	
Review sales skills for field sales staff		High	1 week then quarterly	

Activities to start or increase	Activities to reduce or eliminate	Priority	Timescale	Who
	Stop involvement at trade shows	Medium	Immediate. Review yearly	
Increase tele-marketing and direct mail activities by 20%		High	1 month. Review in 3 months	
Test advertising in specialist trade journals	Stop local press advertising	Medium	Immediate. Review yearly	
Meet with each supplier to review prices based on growth plans		Medium	2 months	
Write one extra editorial piece each month for trade journal		High	1 month. Review quarterly	
Complete roles & responsibilities questionnaire for all staff. Add findings to strategic plan		High	1 month. Review in 6 months	

Examples of Strategic action steps

Distribution Methods and strategies

Organisations often have several means of distributing their products and services. Your strategic planning needs to take account of the differing requirements of all of your key business stakeholders with the appropriate communication methods for each group. You may distribute your product or service offering exclusively on a direct to end user basis. This is referred to as business to consumer or B to C. Where your primary focus of influence is directed to end-users this is termed a pull strategy.

Alternatively, you may combine direct distribution with trade channel distribution. You influence trade channels through a push strategy. This is referred to as business-to-business or B to B. Channel distribution is the delivery of your offering via intermediaries. These intermediaries may include wholesalers, retailers, distributors, value added resellers (VAR) and channel partners.

Your strategic plan needs to align the various channels to maximise business opportunities through intermediaries and to minimise conflict between channels.

A broader based profile strategy will seek to influence your overall presence in the market to raise your profile generally.

Case study: Direct mail success for Macallan

Macallan, producers of a whisky brand were new to direct mail at the time of running their highly successful direct mail campaign. They now use direct mail as a regular part of their marketing communications activities. The aim of the campaign was to increase market share and build stronger relationships with existing customers.

The direct mail campaign was run over a Christmas period, which is when sales volumes and competitor activity are at their peak. The mailing comprised 14,000 pieces that consisted of existing customers and a mailing list that came from a lifestyle survey. The offer included a £1 off voucher. A questionnaire was enclosed for relationship building purposes. The headline read, "If you don't ask for Macallan this Christmas, you'll get the same pair of boring socks".

The campaign produced an astonishing 58% from existing customers and 39% from the cold mailing list.
Source: Royal Mail website—www.royalmail.com

A communications planning framework

A planning framework can assist you to establish effective marketing communications for your organisation overall and with each of your various methods of distribution. The following is an outline of a communications planning framework:

Element	Description
Key business drivers	The social-economic environment. Market conditions and trends. Global influences and other research findings
Communication objectives	What you want to achieve by way of the right messages to the right audience
Promotional strategy	The development of corporate and product brands
Co-ordinated marketing methods	The appropriate blend of marketing activities
Project and resource management	Consideration of timescales and budgets
Review process	Control, evaluation and Refinement

A marketing communications planning framework

Creating your own business peaks

Every business has natural cycles that take it through peaks and troughs. These are created by seasonal and market trends, the economy, competitor activity and other such factors. On an extreme basis, they create feast and famine situations putting severe strain on the well being of the business. It can become extremely problematic to manage resources effectively and systematically. The following diagram illustrates the effect of these natural cycles:

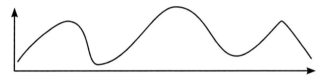

Natural peaks and troughs during a business cycle

Whilst this phenomenon can never be completely eradicated it can be improved substantially. *Through innovation, highly effective and vigorous marketing, the natural peaks and troughs of your business can be raised and flattened.* The next diagram illustrates the positive effect that this can have:

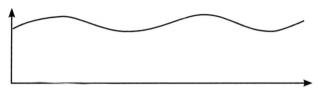

Raise and flatten your business cycle

Creating a Marketing Plan

There are many different methods for creating a marketing plan. The following table is based on the 7Ps formula:

Aspect	Description
Product	A matrix of all your products and services together with product life cycle and sales cycle
People	Knowledge, experience and skills of all staff. Role descriptions and training needs analysis
Place	How you distribute your products and services. Your target market, customer profile and niche markets
Price	Your pricing policy and philosophy

Aspect	Description
Promotion	Promotional mix used to create awareness and generate sales. This includes advertising, direct marketing, sales promotions, personal selling and public relations. Market trends.
Processes	Market research, competitor/SWOT analysis, financial management of marketing budget, ongoing review and refinement process
Physical evidence	Tools, materials and collaterals needed to create the required perception with customers or distributors. Your differentiators and Unique Selling Proposition (USP)

The 7 Ps marketing plan

Sales and marketing audit process

Periodically it is prudent to have a review of your sales and marketing plans, processes and activities. This can be conducted in the form of a sales and marketing audit and can be conducted internally or more objectively by commissioning an external source to carry it out. The following outline provides a list of the key elements to be included in the audit process:

- Market research
  - Key target markets
  - Competitor activity
- Product range
- Sales staff
  - Resource requirements
  - Productivity/Performance and skills
  - Pay and reward system
- Business partnerships/alliances/channels
- Operating territory
- Pricing policy and funding for customer purchases
- Promotional elements
  - Marketing materials
  - Campaign materials
  - Promotional mix/methods

- ◆ Relationship management
- • Monitoring systems/evaluation methods
  - ◆ Sales activity and success ratios
  - ◆ Skill refinement
  - ◆ Prospect management
  - ◆ Campaign management

Other variations of business plan

There are many variations of business plans that can be used for different purposes. I have concentrated on producing an overall strategy plan and a marketing strategy, as these are your key business drivers. You may, however, wish to produce other specialist plans. The following provides examples of other useful planning tools:

Type of Plan	Purpose
Strategic plan	Overall means of establishing, communicating and fulfilling your business objectives
Marketing plan	Processes and activities that link your offering with customers, suppliers and other business stakeholders
Sales plan	Tactical means of achieving sales results. May include separate plan for each product and service offering or vertical market
Operational plan	List of action steps required at operational level to achieve strategic objectives
Traditional business plan	Often used for raising capital. Typically contains: • Executive summary • Purpose of business • Key personnel • Competitive strengths and weaknesses • Funding requirements • Cash flow forecast • Profit and loss statement

Type of Plan	Purpose
Business continuity plan	Used to plan for a catastrophe occurring within your business, such as fire, flood or some other emergency. A good plan aids disaster recovery and determines how your business would survive in times of crisis.

Various types of business plan

Case study: Re-launching Magnum in the UK and Australia

A £25 million advertising campaign was used by Unilever to re-launch their Magnum ice cream brand. This was in response to falling sales and fierce competition from Nestle, Unilever's main competitor.

The campaign theme of "Seven Deadly Sins" was mostly targeted at women encouraging indulgence. An extensive advertising campaign was used on TV and in cinemas. In Australia sales results were 400 per cent above target.

Source: The Times, 6 March 2003.

"The price of greatness is responsibility"—Winston Churchill

Interview with
Kriss Akabusi

What does success mean to Kriss Akabusi?

I have been asked many times in my life what success means to me and to define success. I like to define success as the life you lead, the lessons you learn and the legacy you leave. We have all got our different ethics and morals and values as to the way we live our lives, but when we live our values we have an opportunity to educate or divulge that to other people. So I talk about the life that you lead. What sort of life do you lead? What are the lessons you have learned from your life? Over the last few years I have publicly spoken about lessons I have learned from life and in so doing hoping that you leave a legacy. One thing is for sure. Yesterday you were born and tomorrow you will die and in between is that dash and that dash is on your tombstone representing your life and so, in that life, do you leave a legacy?

When did you first realise you had the potential to be an Olympic and World Champion?

As a young boy at school I was a bit of a gladiator. I played in all the sports. I played football and basketball but I wasn't that good at any of them, purely because I was not focussed. I realised that I had some sort of sporting ability when I joined the army and there was a particular person called Sargent McKenzie who really identified my potential. He was the first person who called me aside and talked about my potential, developed a training programme for me, stayed by my side and gave me my first pair of running spikes. Over that year I went from being an also ran at school to being the army junior champion and that was really my first step on the path of success as far as track and field athletics was concerned.

What are the qualities that create winners in sport and life?

An overriding passionate goal, something that really fires you up, that is in the marrow of your bones and gets you up in the morning. Without that sort of goal it is very difficult to achieve some sort of success. Once you have that sort of goal, you have to understand why is that important to me? Is it about recognition? Is it about reward or about contribution? It is about really understanding that reason why. When you have got the goal and you have got the why, you will find a how very easily. People come around you, you begin to talk about it, you are passionate about it and people key into that passion and the strengths that you have are then complimented by other people's strengths and then you get your success.

Do spectators always appreciate the dedication behind sporting success?

All sportsmen and women's success is very public and it looks fantastic and very easy, but actually, when I became the European Champion for example in 1990, the headlines in the paper the very next day were, 'Akabusi, an overnight success'! It had taken me fifteen years of dedication, training, working very hard to be the very best I could be in my particular arena. Anyone can do a lap of honour, anyone can put on their spikes, but not many people can do the work over the fifteen years required to cross that line first and get the gong around your neck.

What are the emotions after winning at the highest level?

When you have achieved something at world class level and you have really achieved your dream and when you are standing there and you have just been crowned the World champion, Olympic champion, or European champion, the first thing for me is a very disappointing moment. First of all you are on your rostrum. You have given your sample, you are back in your room and you are on your own with four walls and it is like, that's it! The very next morning you are back planning and preparing for the next year and the next assault. It is not until you have got through that bit, that you begin to get back on track again. When you are back training again you do realise what you have done because other people let you know what you have done. It can be a very lonely and dark moment the morning after the night before.

In your presentations what is your message to help people achieve?

When I am speaking to organisations and speaking to people, my keynote speech is about focus, innovation and teamwork but actually what I am trying to do is help people connect with their story, their past and their future and recognise that the moment is now and this moment now is going to send you on your trajectory. When I talk about stories, people connect with their own story and what I like to do is with my poetry, my philosophy and my story telling I link with people so people recognise my story and their story. The story must be true and I am going to make it happen, so it's all about story telling. Focus, innovation, teamwork and making life happen!

What are the sorts of successes you have helped people achieve?

That's one of the pleasures of what I do. I have had phenomenal success inasmuch as I have had women, men, young and old come up to me saying, 'You know, I was at that conference and my boss is not going to like it but when I left I started this new business', or, 'I decided what really mattered to me was my children' so yes, people do connect with their own story and who they are. I like to say that they are the CEO of making their own life happen. It is fantastic when you recognise that you have made that sort of a difference in someone's life.

Why do many people fail to achieve their full potential?

I think that the biggest thing that stops people achieving things is the word 'apathy'. People think, 'well that is for someone else to do'. But often those people that do have the dream and want to follow it come across a wall of fear that comes up in front of them and begins to block out their dream. There was a woman called Helen Keller who was blind. She was a great writer, author and poet and what she said was, 'Face the sun and the shadows of your life will fall behind you'. So what you look at grows in your life and what you hold onto becomes your life and many people hold onto the wall of fear. All the reasons why they can't do something rather than going over to the other side of the fear where their real life really is.

Does society make it harder for young people to achieve success in life?

Yes it is very difficult. I look at the modern world that we live in and in the modern world our young people seem to have everything and yet often have very little. One of the sad things in life was shown through the idea of sport where children are not supposed to compete, and winning and losing is not very good for a young person. I see that being percolated through to the young adults that come into our generation because they don't want to lose and yet, in life, you have to lose because losing is a part of winning. Failure is a part of success and young people today don't want to step into the arena and fail because all of a sudden they feel that they as individuals are failing.

Actually, the human race has got where it is today because it has failed and learned how to control the environment so that it does not fail again. So actually I do feel sorry for the young people in this world. Often, their self esteem is so fragile that one loss means that they are finished when actually one loss should be the antidote to future success.

In hard times what carries you through?

People look at me and I am happy-go-lucky. I am laughing and smiling and I have this great big loud laugh and they think, 'right on, we like that.' But actually I do get dark and dingy moments and I do get depressive moments and, for me, that melancholy is a fantastic sign which tells me that something great is about to happen. In my dark, depressive moments, I begin to ask myself serious questions about who am I, who do I really want to be, what is the true nature of me trying to get out? In that contemplative dark moment, I begin to ask myself those questions and the new me begins to emerge and from the cocoon becomes the new being, the new butterfly that is going to show up on stage. That is a great moment for me. I don't run away from those dark moments; I contemplate, I think and I ask myself the real questions in life.

What books have inspired and helped you?

There are so many books that have inspired me over the last fifteen years or so. I became an avid reader in 1987 and the catalyst for that was my faith. I was in Edinburgh and it was good news for me as it was in plain English and I read that from cover to cover and I met this man called Jesus the Nazarene and that really spawned my reading and so, the very first book on my hit list would be *The Bible*. It is the Good News bible because it is in very simple plain language and it spoke to me in my vernacular but it really spawned a hunger and thirst for knowledge.

The next book I would recommend is *The Classics of Western Thought* and the publisher is HBJ. In that book from ancient antiquity to the modern world, they give you clips of the classics such as Voltaire and Russo and you engage with these minds and you see all the contemporary stuff that is going on and realise it has all happened before. You see the fundamentals of these thoughts and that was fantastic for me. All of a sudden I understood how institutions came together, the social contract and all that sort of stuff. It really opened my mind and spawned more and more reading.

I am African by birth and yet I am very British; I speak English, I have got a British mentality and I began to ask myself about how I have got here and so the third book was the *African Diaspora* by Ronald Segal. I began to read about the African slave trade and black men and women came to this country and the contribution they have made over the last 500 years and that again was a rude awakening for me to understand that, OK I am here in this country legitimately and I am allowed to make a contribution.

What goals do you still have?

When you stop dreaming and having goals you are dead and it won't be too long before you are! My next goal is to be a catalyst for change in the country of my origin and that is Nigeria. I was born in this country, my parents come from Nigeria. I have been to Nigeria and I have seen the good things in the country and I have seen the many bad things and as I go to rural communities I look at some of those children. I see boys and girls who look like they are six and seven years old and actually they are fifteen or sixteen years old but they have stunted growth. I look at the water they drink. Water which is supposed to give life is full of cholera and typhoid and all these things that bring death. So I have recognised that my goal is to make a massive contribution to that country. By 2008 I will be six months of the year contributing to the rural development and the community health.

How would you like to be remembered?

I would like to be remembered by that dash on my tombstone to represent someone who was Passionate, Energetic and left a Legacy.

||||||||||||||||||||||||||||||||||||||||||||||||||||||||||||||||||||||

Kriss Akabusi is famous for his achievements in athletics where his greatest individual triumph was his Gold Medal in the 1990 European Championships when he also beat David Hemery's 22-year old British Record.

From 1992 to 1998 Kriss's TV career began with a period as presenter of *The Big Breakfast* which was quickly followed by a full time position as co-host of the BBC'S flagship programme *Record Breakers*.

Kriss is currently the CEO of The Akabusi Company, a corporate communications and training company where his marvellous personality and reputation as a fantastic public speaker has made him a very popular and attractive advocate.

⁞⁞

Watch this video interview plus many more like it through your free subscription to online business TV portal Expertsonline.tv available to you as a buyer of this book. Just send an e-mail to **info@expertsonline.tv**, *including the ISBN number, and the location of where you bought the book to receive your free subscription worth £50.*

Chapter 4

Winning in an increasingly competitive world

"There is one quality that one must possess to win, and that is definiteness of purpose, the knowledge of what one wants and a burning desire to achieve it" —Napoleon Hill

Managing our tasks and managing our relationships with others on a daily basis is incredibly challenging. How is it that some people manage to achieve their desired outcomes and enjoy the process? In this chapter we will consider techniques to assist us in the way we manage time and other resources. Ultimately, we all have the same 24 hours in a day. Unlike other commodities, we cannot borrow from time or reuse it once it has passed. We need to make each second count whilst enjoying the moment.

We need to make each second count whilst enjoying the moment.

Aligning personal and business goals

The more the personal goals of your people are aligned with your business goals, the greater your probability of success. To ignore the personal goals of your people is a big blunder. To understand how closely matched individual and business goals are is a significant strategic advantage. This does not mean that you force your business objectives into your people's personal lives. On the contrary, by understanding and tracking business and personal goals you are able to make business decisions that are more likely to succeed long term.

Let's take an example. If you know that one of your key people is planning to leave over the next year to set up in business with their spouse, you can plan various options in advance as to how best to replace them. If, alternatively, you are ignorant of this information and you receive one month's notice of their leaving, this could leave you in a frantic position.

This does not mean that you pry into your people's personal lives. If you are prepared to share your personal and business goals with your team and create a vision, then they are more likely to want to share information with you. *A healthy philosophy in building teams is to find, to grow and to send your people.* Sometimes this means happily letting go of your best people for them to reach greater heights in their own personal quest for success. It requires you to have their best interests at heart.

By sharing personal and business goals you achieve greater clarity towards a combined vision. This is expressed in the following diagrams.

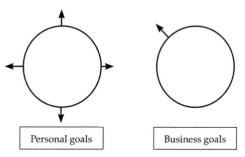

| Personal goals | Business goals |

Separate non-communicated personal and business goals

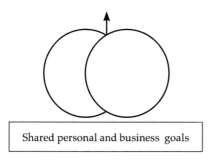

Shared personal and business goals

A shared common vision

Managing change

Your organisation will be constantly ebbing and flowing as both external and internal influences take effect. A natural seasonal uplift will create activity and growth, whilst the loss of a key member of your team will be unsettling. While there is a limit to the extent of control you have on many factors, you always have control over how you respond to changing circumstances. Change is inevitable; however, growth is a matter of choice. We have to make a conscious decision to grow through change. Change is occurring constantly and incessantly. It is occurring at micro and at macro level. It is occurring in our business and personal lives. The following diagram demonstrates the four phases of change.

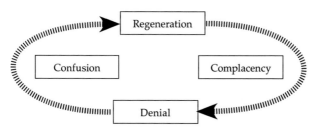

Four phases of change

---

*You always have control over
how you respond to changing
circumstances.*

Regeneration: This is a growth period when we are building and developing opportunities. We are focused, active and making progress towards our goals. We are able to operate decisively and manage challenges as they occur.

Complacency: At some stage we start to lose focus and become distracted. We reduce the level of concentration and determined effort that we had applied previously. Things start to go wrong and opportunities are missed. This happens slowly at first and approaches very discretely. The perception is that all is well and we can rest on our laurels.

Denial: Larger problems begin to occur and we still ignore the warning signs. We deny that there is anything wrong and we refuse to take personal responsibility. It is too late at this stage to create immediate remedies. Problems need to be solved at a higher level of thinking than when they were created. New solutions are now required but at this stage we are not prepared to consider them. Eventually we realise the scale of chaos around us and start to panic.

Confusion: We become stressed and confused. This is often associated with feelings of despair and helplessness. We find it difficult to make decisions and we are reluctant to tackle new tasks. This can be combined with a loss of personal identity, becoming insular and a general withdrawal of communicating with others.

Completing the circle: We accept our shortcomings we modify our behaviour and we start to grapple with the issues. We make plans. We become inspired. Finally we move on and start to grow again.

Awareness: Being aware of the four phases of change enables us to operate at a higher level of consciousness. Whilst we cannot vary the order of movement from one phase to the next nor stop the movement altogether, we can alter the pace of change. Through conscious effort we can slow it down and we can speed it up.

While we are enjoying a period of regeneration we can be ever watchful of becoming complacent. We can continue to apply consistent determined effort. We can recognise the early signs of exaggerated contentment. We can refine our goals and redouble our efforts. We can maintain a sharp focus and remain alert. We can remain active and decisive whilst avoiding any temptation to become lethargic.

Once complacency strikes we can consciously accept our situation, review our options and take an alternative course of action. We can seek advice and counsel from others. We can keep our spirits raised in the knowledge that we can handle the challenges that stand before us. We can speed up our recovery. We can be searching for and open to our next opportunity for growth.

Effective time management

You are able to assess the value of your time by reviewing your past and current activities. You can use this as the driver to plan, prioritise and re-organise your schedule. How you interact with others to manage the time resource within a team is also a key function of effective time management for leaders and managers. The overall objective is to use a number of techniques and strategies to increase productivity. Unfortunately, just stopping your watch doesn't help!

How critical is your time?

When was the last time you paused to consider how critical your time is and how this relates to people in different circumstances? Think about the following:

- The difference a *day* makes to the busy executive completing a report to the Board
- The difference an *hour* makes to the expectant parent waiting for the birth of their first baby
- The difference a *minute* makes to the commuter who just missed a train

- The difference a *second* makes to the driver who just missed a collision with another vehicle
- The difference a *millisecond* makes to the Olympic runner who came second in the race

---

*Each day is the building block of
our life and our future.*

For us to make a difference to our lives and others we need to respect our time and other peoples time. We all have the same twenty-four hours in a day to achieve our mission. Each day is the building block of our life and our future. We can create considerable rewards by isolating what really matters to us and spending our time working towards these desires.

The benefits of effective time management

Our daily time resource can be considered a credit of 86,400 seconds. As each new day arrives we receive our next block of credit into our time bank account. We each receive the same daily credit of time and with this credit comes responsibility. Just like cash resources, we can choose to invest our time wisely or fritter it away foolishly. Unlike cash resources however, we cannot create it, store it, borrow from it nor recover lost time. Whether we want to or not, we are forced to spend the same sum each and every day. Managing our time is therefore our most critical task. We receive immense benefits from the effective use of time. Some of these benefits include:

- Being more productive at work and at leisure
- Leading a less stressful life
- Feeling more in control

Putting a value on our time at work

Most of us underestimate our value at work. We can make a quick calculation of our value using a simple formula, as follows:

Value per hour   = $$\frac{\text{Annual income x overhead factor}}{\text{Hours worked per annum}}$$

The overhead factor is the element of additional cost associated with our role in order for us to receive the income. This includes items such as direct taxation and running costs such as heating, lighting and rates.

For example, we will assume an overhead factor of 2, hours per week of 35 and number of working weeks as 48. Each £10,000 of annual income results in the following value per hour:

$$\frac{20,000 \ (10,000 \times 2)}{1,680 \ (35 \times 48)}$$

This equates to *£11.90* (20,000 / 1,680) per hour for every £10,000 of annual income.

Listing our most valuable tasks

Here is an exercise for you to list your most valuable tasks. Make a list of each important task that requires your attention on a regular basis. Here is an initial list to help you get started:

- Time spent serving customers (Including colleagues and employees who are also your customers)
- Time prospecting for new customers and recruiting staff
- Setting short and long term goals (personal and work related)
- Planning your time
- Time with family friends
- Hobbies

> *The shadow by my finger cast*
> *Divides the future from the past*
> *Behind its unrelenting line,*
> *The vanished hour no longer thine.*

> *Before it lies the unknown hour.*
>   *In darkness and beyond thy power.*
> *One hour alone is in thy hands.*
>   *The now on which the shadow stands.*

The shadow

Case study

A vehicle rentals company whose IT systems were not integrated and wanted to increase business through the Internet. A thorough analysis of their existing systems was carried out and the company were presented with proposals to replace some of the existing systems and integrate them more fully. They now have an integrated solution with up-to-date information on their fleet and its availability. Their website has been redeveloped to make it more user-friendly and an Internet marketing campaign is currently under way.

The importance of keeping records

In order for you to appreciate how much time you spend with various tasks you need to keep records. If this is not already part of your daily discipline then on a regular basis you can complete an activity log. The activity log needs to be completed over a reasonable time frame say one to two weeks, divided into thirty-minute time segments. This will provide you with an analysis of exactly where you are spending your time. You can then use this to make refinements to your daily routine.

You will want to categorise your activity log into groups. The following examples may help:

1. Activities essential to productivity
2. Essential but not productive activities
3. Not essential

The following is a sample activity log that has been divided into thirty-minute segments:

Date:

Time	Activity
5:00	
5:30	
6:00	
6:30	
7:00	
7:30	
8:00	
8:30	
9:00	
9:30	
10:00	
10:30	
11:00	
11:30	
12:00	
12:30	
1:00	
1:30	
2:00	
2:30	
3:00	
3:30	
4:00	
4:30	
5:00	
5:30	

Time	Activity
6:00	
6:30	
7:00	
7:30	
8:00	
8:30	
9:00	
9:30	
10:00	
10:30	
11:00	
11:30	
12:00	
12:30	
1:00	

Time Analysis

Once you have completed your activity log you are then able to perform analysis and make comparisons against your objectives. The table below includes suggested objectives:

Category	Time Spent	Objective
1	Essential and productive	60%
2	Essential not productive	25%
3	Not essential	15%

Time analysis table

Qualities of an effective time manager

An effective time manager is motivated towards being productive. They are constantly looking for time saving opportunities and refinements to processes that improve effectiveness. They manage their energy levels to ensure that tasks are completed consistently and to high quality standards. They maintain focus on the task in hand rather than getting distracted by less essential elements.

When a task needs to be done by them they deal with it immediately. They have a do-it-now philosophy. Effective time managers are committed to completing what they set out to achieve and within agreed timescales. They refine their skills and obtain the qualifications they need to ensure competence in their chosen field.

> *Effective time managers are committed to completing what they set out to achieve and within agreed timescales.*

The process of planning

There are a number of techniques you can use to assist with the planning process for all tasks. Start by completing your activity log. This identifies where your time is being spent and enables you to review your priorities. It will provide for you a guide of activities that you want to increase and others that you want to decrease.

You can block out time slots in your diary or planner to accommodate key tasks that need to take place. Apart from appointments involving other people you can also schedule appointments with yourself to undertake dedicated tasks. For example, you may want to block out specific time for business development, personal reading, preparation and thinking time.

Taking larger activities and breaking them down into more manageable chunks can achieve incredible results.

Major tasks can sometimes seem extremely complex and never ending. By breaking them down and tackling each element separately you are able to move progressively towards completion and a successful outcome.

Prioritisation

There are three main categories of urgency that can be further broker down into sub-categories. The three main categories are:

1.   Tasks that are urgent and important
2.   Tasks that are either urgent or important
3.   Task that are neither urgent nor important

Mixing all three categories throughout the day will enable you to deal with any emergencies as they occur whilst balancing the need to develop longer-term important essentials. Set priorities and work through activities in their order of priority. Priorities can be time-based and they can also be based on the relative importance of a task. The following is a suggested list of priorities starting from the most important to the least important:

1.   Must be completed or serious consequences will result
2.   Needs to be completed
3.   Would be nice if it could be completed
4.   Needs to be delegated to someone else
5.   Could be completed but has no real consequences

Prioritising tasks

Urgent and important? NO YES	Need to complete today? NO YES	Take immediate action
Urgent or important? NO YES	Is there a deadline? NO YES	Set aside time to complete
		Set realistic deadline
Is it routine? NO YES	Help you work more effectively? NO YES	Allocate time to complete
Discard	Is it necessary? NO YES	Save till quiet time

Dealing with the urgent and the important

Working with others

Do you allow others in your team constantly to interrupt your working day? Do you interrupt others yourself? Allocating specific times during the day to discuss issues with your team members avoids the problem of constant interruptions. Let others in your team know that you are available only between certain times of the day. Have your external calls filtered where possible.

When copying information to others, consider who really needs it and only provide it to those individuals. Arrange meetings only if really necessary. Generally, a 'phone call is a more efficient use of time. Always have objectives for 'phone calls and meetings. Spend more time listening than talking. Start and finish on time. If travelling, plan your journey and combine nearby visits where possible. Make a list of topics to be discussed or have an agenda. *Practise the principles of Discussion, Decision and Action.* Ensure that you follow up on your agreed action points. Delegate tasks where possible.

Delegating tasks

It is always good practise to look at any task and to consider the question as to why it should be you that completes the task. Good leaders concentrate on conducting the tasks that only they can do. You might like to consider what particular skills, knowledge or qualifications are required to complete the task. You may decide that someone other than you is best placed to carry out the task. By reviewing the task you may decide that it is of a low priority and should be deferred for another time.

Good leaders concentrate on conducting the tasks that only they can do.

Here is a useful technique for handling tasks in a leadership or supervisory capacity:

Do	The task needs to be completed and you are the best person to do it
Delegate	The task needs to be completed but someone else is equally or better equipped to handle it
Dump	The task has no real consequences and can be deferred for now

Delegating a task does not mean devolving yourself of the responsibility of the successful completion of the task. You retain the responsibility and by having a reporting process you are able to check on progress being made.

Maintaining a master list

It is good practise to become somewhat of a list fanatic. Rather than producing several different lists for different aspects of your life, you may want to keep one master "to do" list for daily tasks. Each item can include priority level and deadline date. By completing the most difficult and challenging tasks first, you are able to give yourself a productivity boost. Much satisfaction can be gained by completing difficult tasks. By getting them out of the way, you are then able to concentrate on less demanding tasks that may be more enjoyable. Remember, it is only in a dictionary that play comes before work! Build into your schedule the need for preparation time and adequate follow up time. Don't forget to include adequate thinking time. Review and refresh the list daily.

By completing the most difficult and challenging tasks first, you are able to give yourself a productivity boost.

Staying organised

You can remain organised by continually reviewing your master list as new information becomes available. Consider your energy peaks and troughs throughout the day. If you are more energetic in the morning, then aim to complete the most energy draining tasks early on in the day. Maintain high and consistent energy levels with regular breaks, including food breaks and rest breaks. Use one-hour spurts of activity. This enables you to remain focused and productive. When you are working on several different concurrent tasks you can use sequencing to constantly manage each task and keep them moving. Reward yourself on the completion of significant tasks.

Organising material to work with

Attempt to deal with one item at a time and deal with it only once. Keep everything else away from your desk space. If you use filing trays these can be labelled In, Out, Pending and Filing. Filing can be separated into three different sections depending upon how frequently the information needs to be retrieved. For example, regular retrieval items, infrequent use items and archived items can all be filed separately. Keep regular items filed nearer to you.

Be ruthless by only retaining items that are required for reference purposes and dump the rest. Use colour markers to identify different groups of materials. Become proficient at skim reading and highlighting key text. When you are producing new materials use mind-mapping techniques to maximise your creative thinking processes.

In summary, be aware of the value of your time. Plan your activity using a master to do list. Have clear goals and objectives. Monitor where you spend your time. Keep refining skills and methods to improve how well you are organised and how you can communicate with others more effectively.

Working with the media

Developing relationships with the press, radio and television contacts will pay big dividends. Much free publicity is to be gained by nurturing these influential contacts. Success in business is more to do with whom you know rather than what you know. For example, most paid-for local newspapers have specialised sections that require to be filled on a regular basis with the appropriate copy. This is a perfect opportunity to write informative material that you can submit as an article.

Whilst you may not have the budget to spend on a national television commercial, do not rule out television altogether. There are numerous regional, cable and specialist channels where the cost may be within your reach. Television is particularly well suited to mass market consumable products or services. If you have an easily described offering with a broad appeal, then television advertising could work well for you. For example, simple insurance products may be suited to this method of advertising.

As with all types of advertising you need to ensure that you communicate a message that has already been proven to generate enquiries. Do not waste expensive advertising budgets by using untested materials. Some degree of targeting can also be achieved based on the various broadcast regions throughout the UK. The timing of your advertisement will also have a link to the demographics of your audience. For example, advertise Saturday mornings to reach children of school age for the promotion of toys and junior magazines.

Radio advertising is often overlooked by businesses today. There are approximately two hundred independent local radio stations in the UK. Typically, forty percent of the population tune in to local stations with the highest number of listeners on Sunday mornings. This gives you an opportunity to reach a large proportion of the local population with a high impact message. Radio advertising is substantially cheaper than television advertising.

Media strategies

If you have a particularly newsworthy message that you want to communicate to the marketplace then you will want choose the most effective method. For example you may want to promote, a new breakthrough innovation that offers benefits to a broad range of people. This could be achieved with an appropriate news release or series of releases. Construct your news releases using the following criteria:

- Identify your target audience
- Gain the appropriate media contacts
- Ensure you watch, listen and read appropriate materials on an ongoing basis

- Use a media friendly format (as apposed to a traditional writing format)

Traditional writing is significantly different to the format used in news releases. Tradition writing will often include an introduction, followed by brief context, then more detailed background, related history and finally a conclusion. News releases on the other hand use the opposite approach, as the following diagram illustrates:

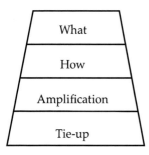

The "What" triangle

The "what" triangle approach to writing attracts interest and sets the scene quickly by establishing the "what", "where", "why" and "when" elements at the start. These are all the key facts and circumstances. This is followed by more detailed explanation with the "how" and "amplification". The tie-up provides a brief summary and includes any loose ends that have been missed. Using this format, the bulk of the story remains intact even if the Editor has to cut the article or feature short due to space restrictions.

What makes news?

The majority of reported stories tend to cover negative situations. It is for this reason that your association with a story has to be carefully managed. This requires a cautious approach in order to avoid potential damage to your reputation and that of your business. In order to attract interest it is acceptable to be outspoken, thought provoking, opinionated and even eccentric. You however need to ensure that you stop short of becoming outrageous or by shocking your potential audience. Your relationships with the media therefore need to be managed with mutual respect and professionalism. The following areas cover the most topical news items:

- Scandal (often linked to sex, drugs or money)
- People (something out of the ordinary)
- Novelty (new, different or better)
- Conflict (high impact factor: challenge, disagreement and drama)
- Community (particular opportunities, dangers or threats to society)
- Event (major or unusual events)

Interviews with the media

Interviews covered in the press and on radio or television provide a major opportunity for you to raise your profile and gain publicity. Always ensure that you are fully prepared before you speak and avoid spontaneous interviews. Be clear about your knowledge of the subject and whether you are the right person to speak on the subject. You will only have a limited time to get your message across. Live interviews typically last for approximately three minutes duration (approximately 400 words). Always choose face-to-face interviews in preference to telephone interviews where possible. This enables you to reinforce your message with the appropriate body language. The following table gives additional guidance:

Aspect	Guidance
Evaluate	Fully prepare. Be alert, fresh and enthusiastic. Find out in advance what the first question is going to be.
Investigate	Do your research beforehand and check your facts.
Eliminate	Be specific and ruthless with your material. Only focus on a few key messages. Get your key points in early. Know when to shut up.

Aspect	Guidance
Illustrate	Find human-interest stories and examples to make key points. Avoid jargon
Orchestrate	Stay on track. Think of questions you can pose to the interviewer. Consider what words that you want to avoid. Watch out for leading questions. Don't be intimidated

Interviews with the media

Crisis management

There may be a need to manage the media during a business crisis. In this situation it is appropriate to control the crisis and not let the crisis control you. During times of crisis it is important you continue to manage a relationship with the media by establishing:

- Trust and credibility
- An expression of concern for the current situation
- Responsibility for handling the situation

This is a crucial time to ensure that your staff are kept informed of developments. You need to appoint a leader to manage the situation and a spokesperson responsible for communications both inside your organisation and externally. You may also require a team of experts to resolve the issues.

When dealing with the media, always focus on the relevant facts and avoid speculation. Produce a holding statement in writing that you can distribute. Do not get drawn into speculative scenarios, just say, "I have nothing more to add right now".

Interview with
Max Clifford

What does success mean to Max Clifford?

I suppose it's fulfilment. It's basically being able to do the things in life that you most want to do, and you don't need anybody else to do it. Success is that for me. It means basically that if I really want something for myself or the family, I can afford it. In terms of the quality of life, you are able to control it. So as far as possible, success for me has meant that I'm able to fulfil myself without needing anybody else. So I've been extremely lucky, but that is how I would quantify that fulfilment. Success means that you can do it and you can do it your own way, when you want to and without needing to get help from anybody else, and that's a wonderful position to be in. I suppose it maximises your self-efficiency, the fact that you're able to achieve the things in life that are most important to you without anyone else being needed to help you do it.

You have reached the top of your profession. How ambitious were you at the outset?

I didn't really have any ambition other than to enjoy myself. And touch wood, I've always managed to do that. I suppose I'm naturally competitive, so whenever I took on any client—that is a star, an organisation, or an aspiring star or whatever—you want to show that you can do it better than anybody else. And fortunately for me I was around at the right time. I mean for me; it was the 60s, I had just joined EMI having been a local reporter on a local paper, joined EMI Press Office no one had heard of public relations. So I was able to learn at a time when it was okay, you made mistakes, well fine. There was no one to teach you because the public relations industry hadn't even started. We were just press officers. So I think it was the right time, right place, but it was something that came very naturally to me. So I didn't have any ambitions other than to do whatever I did better than anybody else, and to enjoy myself, and fortunately I managed to combine the two most of the time.

How much does luck play a part in success?

You show me anybody that has had success to any degree and I'll show you someone that's had a bit of luck along the way. That was a huge slice of luck for me. The fact is I'd just joined the press office at EMI, I was 19 years old, it was 1962 and I was given an unknown band to help launch— The Beatles and *Love Me Do*. So it was the right time and the right place and I was just incredibly lucky because with their success, which happened so quickly world-wide, it meant that I had built contacts throughout the media world wide. No way was it down to Max Clifford; it was down to their success. I reaped the enormous benefits of being part of that. And of course in any industry, nothing succeeds like success—'Oh he must be good because he's working with The Beatles'. Well you could have been the village idiot because they did it all themselves, but it meant that the media from all over the world in the early days, if they wanted information, any details of what was going on in and around the careers of The Beatles, they had to come to Max Clifford at the EMI press office. So, you know, it was a wonderful kick start and obviously it put me right in the centre of things from day one.

How exciting was that period of your life?

It was exciting. I must tell you that EMI had turned down The Beatles once, and people know that Decca turned them down. Very few people realised that the same demo tape that they submitted to Decca was turned down by EMI. It was a rock and roll tape singing Fats Domino, Jerry Lee Lewis and Chuck Berry songs. And then Brian Epstein came along and fell in love with John Lennon, submitted a tape of Lennon and McCartney songs and I think they just about passed it at the Board at EMI. I remember at the time we were launching *Love Me Do* with the then

Marketing Director of EMI taking me to one side and saying don't waste any time on this lot son, they've got no chance. True story. And of course a year later when they were celebrating huge success, Ron was there shaking their hands and saying, 'I always knew you were going to be the ones'. That's just another lesson; back your own judgement, forget everybody else, follow your instincts.

What were the other breaks you got in the 60s?

I think it was the element of luck all the way from the start, inasmuch as most of the people that I was involved with right at the beginning. I mean I was at EMI and it just so happened that we had a whole feast of great clients coming through. We had Cliff and Adam Faith emerging, The Beatles came along and then all of the Liverpool lads off the back of that; Jerry and the Pacemakers etc. And then within a short space of time Smoky Robinson; they came over from Detroit and EMI licensed and then distributed Tamla Motown. So we launched over here and in Europe: The Jackson Five, Diana Ross, Marvin Gaye, Stevie Wonder, The Four Tops, The Temptations, so it was an amazing time. Just about everything we touched turned to gold. And the other wonderful thing is that 40 years on they're still household names which I doubt very much you'll be able to say about the current pop in the charts today.

Was it always your aim to set up your own company?

It was never my decision; I've never really mapped out a career at all, it just kind of happened to me. Sid Gillingham who was the Chief press officer at EMI, who introduced me and who basically gave me a job in the first place, he left to form his own company and asked me to go with him. We helped to launch people like Tom Jones, Engelbert Humperdinck, Gilbert O'Sullivan, The BeeGees, Cream and people like that. But it was really under Sid's banner. I was always one of these people that, you know, do my own thing my own way, and because he watched me at EMI and he knew that I'd got results, he just let me do my own thing and I worked best that way. Sid was much too nice at public relations. I mean Sid would be charming to people that were phoning him up in the middle of the night, whereas I would put the phone down and tell them where to go—totally different attitude and mentality. So when Sid decided to call it a day and go back to journalism (he'd previously been a writer on *The Daily Telegraph* I think it was), I was naturally, if you like, on my own. And that was I think about 33 years ago and I was 27 and I started on my own. It happened if you like, because I was put in a situation where you might as well. I had various clients anyway so I just took them with me and started on my own. So there was never a time when I sat down and thought, 'oh, I'm going to start a public relations company'; I didnt have a clue. I left school at the age of 15 with no qualifications and worked for local department store as a trainee salesman until I got the sack. I was bored to tears and totally had the wrong attitude to be serving people. So it just happened, but I think really that most of it's been tho right time and the right place.

What is the secret of effective PR?

I think it's never going to be rocket science. It's basically what do they need and what's the best way of getting it. I suppose as a kid I only ever had one hero and that was a guy called Johnny Haines who played for Fulham. He was the greatest passer of the ball I've probably seen almost to this day. If you think of how heavy the ball used to get in those days as well. But I see my business as providing opportunities for other people to get those goals, and you find the most effective way of breaking down the defence, you know, whatever it is. I mean that's the interesting thing about my business is that there's no two situations the same and it's an ever-changing field. The media is changing all the time. So yes, you've got to get results. But as I said, I'm a very competitive person so I can't take part—I've got to win and I've got to do everything I can to. I'm a terrible loser; it's just my nature unfortunately. I wish

I could be more sportsmanlike but I can't, it just doesn't work.

So I had the practical education in terms of public relations. Nowadays it's all theory and at University it's the second or third most popular degree course all over the country—PR Communications, English, etc., etc. All of the girls, all of the team that work for me have got all kinds of degrees. I didn't get an 'O' level or so much as a certificate for woodwork when I was at school. I found out how to get results. You know, it's a combination of things; you build the contact, you treat people the way you want them to treat you, you understand what they're looking for, you understand how this paper works and that's the kind of angle that will go for them, this paper will want that, this magazine this TV programme. And we work world-wide.

How has your role changed over the years?

Well we still have to promote, but by far the biggest part, particularly the major stars or the major organisations, is protection. Technically, the biggest part of protection is anticipation. Unless I know more about them than anybody else then I can't do the job, and because the media is increasingly savage (the British media), it's like walking through a minefield. And you know, there are so many different ways of getting blown up. So the biggest part of my job, ironically, over the last decade particularly has been keeping things out of the media rather than what you're trying to get in the media.

Situations vary, but are there broad principles to be followed?

Not really. All you've got to ascertain is, it's a bit like a football match' you know, what's gone wrong? And what do you need to do to put it right. It's as simple as that, although often it's a bit more complicated how you achieve it. But the media is my world and the media is increasingly powerful. Whether it's trying to get some kind of propaganda across or it's trying to get justice. I mean I can get justice for ordinary members of the public in a way that the Police can't and the Law Courts can't. And I can give you dozens of examples of how that works, but that is hugely satisfying. If you can tap in to the power of the media then sometimes you can achieve an awful lot that can't be achieved from the kind of areas of society that should be able to take care of things.

Why do you think the Press is so savage today?

We seem to hate success in this country. I mean the media plays a big part in building people up, but very quickly it turns and, you know, people say, you know, look at all these terrible things they read about people in the papers, and constantly people are being slagged off or attacked or destroyed. But if you don't want that kind of press, you don't buy the papers. And the sad fact is that a bad story is far more appealing to the British public than a good story. If I was to put up ten really happy stories that give you a lift—like someone has done something wonderful for someone—then ten stories which are about destruction—exposing someone, humiliating or ruining someone—it's the second lot that the Editors will go for.

What effects have you seen the Press have on ordinary people?

Well it's really difficult because there are more organisations. There are the Press Complaints and people like that who are there to protect members of the public from bad, unfair, unjust and intrusive treatment, but it's a theory. In reality, in my view it doesn't happen. There are people who suddenly get caught into the media spotlight; someone's had a tragic accident or something's happened to a member of their family or whatever and, you know, the press swarm all over them. But there's no one there for them. You see, if you're a star, if you're rich, famous and powerful, you've got tons of protection. You can afford a PR person like myself. If you're immensely rich you can afford lawyers. But the public have got no one. And all the time there's no Legal Aid for libel, they've got no one to stand up for them. And even if they eventually win their claim, what goes in as a small apology on page 48 when it was a front page splash, so no one notices it, no one sees it. But for most people it's impossible. The media can destroy lives, it does destroy lives and the quality of life for lots of people; ordinary members of the public. So one of the things I feel strongly about is that that's an area that should be looked at and should be changed. There should be Legal Aid for libel for ordinary members of the public because that would give them a chance.

So would you advocate a privacy law?

I would be against a privacy law because the plusses outweigh the minuses. I mean, there's a lot of things happened that are totally wrong. There's a lot of times when it's wrong for newspapers to do what they do and write what they do, but the alternative is that a lot of things would not appear that should appear. There's a lot of people, very rich and very powerful that have been shown up to be totally corrupt in this country over the years. We'd never have done that without a free press. So, much as I find revolting a lot of what I see in the papers and in the media, and knowing just how unfairly a lot of people have been treated, it's preferable from the alternative. It's the lesser of the two evils.

Who were the most charismatic people to work with?

Oh well, that's pretty simple. There are two people that would stand out of the people I've worked with over the years of having that kind of magic everywhere they go, and that would have been Frank Sinatra and Mohammed Ali. I've been in different parts of the world with both and they are instantly recognised in countries where they wouldn't recognise the Queen or virtually anybody else. I mean, very different people. Sinatra when he was good could be wonderful but when he was bad he was awful. Whereas Mohammed Ali was a magical man, is a magical man. He is one of the few major superstars who genuinely care about ordinary people. That's remarkably rare. For most stars there's only one person who matters in the world and that's them. Some are better actors than others but most of them are totally full of themselves and when you work as close as I do with them you know it better than anyone. But Mohammed Ali is special. Mohammed Ali would go to a kids' hospital with no publicity and he wouldn't leave until he'd seen everyone there. And he'd come out and he'd be thanking me for taking him and it was genuine. I mean I could tell you a million stories about the man, he's magic.

Paul Newman, another one, a special man. Someone who liked to put back and someone who doesn't take himself too seriously—there's not many stars like that.

But purely for charisma, Sinatra was magic. Mohammed Ali magic. They would be the two popular at the very top of the tree.

Are there any books that are special to you?

Well, as I said, I left school at 15 barely able to read or write, so books wouldn't be a strong point. I suppose *The Moon's a Balloon*, I seem to remember, a biography of Peter Ustinov which I found hugely entertaining and amusing. Dick Francis, for light relief going back a few years. But no, I can't honestly say that there's a book that really for me is the meaning of life and it's really changed my attitude and views, but those are the kind of ones that mostly make me laugh. Because I suppose I work extremely hard, I work seven days a week ritually I suppose, 18 hours a day by virtue of the business that I am in—and that's not a complaint, I love every minute of it. So when I read it's pure relaxation and I love to see the funny things and the great storytellers. It's the same with entertainment; I love the Billy Connollys, I love the raconteurs. I like people that can talk about everyday life but can turn it into something hysterically funny because, you know, we need that. There's enough terrible things going on out there. Laughter along with love is one of the special commodities in my life. And fortunately I found an awful lot of both.

Are there any remaining goals for Max Clifford?

Anybody that can stumble into something—a career, a business by pure chance which they absolutely love and is an adventure, where there is never two days the same, doing it your own way, on your own terms and making a very good living for myself and my family—youve got to say, well, it doesn't really get much better than that. What I do is hugely rewarding, but is hugely rewarding financially *and* spiritually. I get an awful lot out, but I can put an awful lot back as well and I like to do that.

||||||||||||||||||||||||||||||||||||||||||||||||||||||||||||||||||||||||

Max Clifford is one of the world's most successful publicists. He has been in the business of public relations protecting and promoting a wide variety of clients for well over 40 years. He has become as instantly recognisable as many of the stars he has represented over the years. His views and comments are sought on a daily basis for the world's media on a wide range of subjects and he regularly appears on TV and radio as a guest on current affairs, news, documentaries and chat shows.

||||||||||||||||||||||||||||||||||||||||||||||||||||||||||||||||||||||||

Watch this video interview plus many more like it through your free subscription to online business TV portal Expertsonline.tv available to you as a buyer of this book. Just send an e-mail to **info@expertsonline.tv**, *including the ISBN number, and the location of where you bought the book to receive your free subscription worth £50.*

Chapter 5

Managing Customer relationships

"A customer who complains is my best friend."—Stew Leonard

The following table lists key elements of relationship development.

Reliability	Ability to fulfil the promised service dependably and accurately
Responsiveness	Willingness to help customers and provide prompt service
Assurance	Knowledge and courtesy of staff and their ability to inspire trust and confidence
Empathy	Caring, individualism and attention provided to customers
Tangibles	Physical facilities, equipment and appearance of personnel

Customer relationship development

In order for the relationship to develop, any difference between customer expectations and organisational delivery must be addressed. *A quality customer relationship consists of mutual exchange and fulfilment of promises.*

Why you always need to add to your customer base

Some owners of very established businesses believe that they do not need to continue to expand the size of their customer base. This is a mistake due to natural customer attrition. If you are not constantly and actively marketing for new customers, the size of your customer base will decline with time. Circumstances change, people move, people die, competitors attack and your customer base will decline. This is not an area to be complacent.

In order for the relationship to develop, any difference between customer expectations and organisational delivery must be addressed.

The graph below illustrates the effect of a 10% compounding of your customer base either increasing (growth) or decreasing (attrition). In just five years, your turnover and profits can either more than double or literally shrink to just over half their current size. You choose!

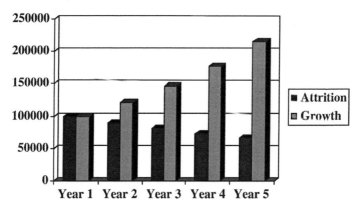

Risk & reward of active customer development

Finding and developing quality customers

It is important to make the distinction between prospective customers and just suspects. True prospects and quality customers need to meet specific criteria in order to establish a mutually beneficial relationship. By having set criteria for an ideal customer, you are able to profile exactly the type of customer that you want. When marketing to prospects you are able to focus on attracting customers that meet your ideal profile. For existing customers you are able to segment your customer base into grades of customers. You can reward your best customers through loyalty programmes and you can nurture your less profitable customers into becoming more productive.

By having set criteria for an ideal customer, you are able to profile exactly the type of customer you want.

The following is a list of four key factors that can be used to assess true customer value and provides a means of profiling your ideal customer:

1. There must be a *need* for the product or service you are providing
2. You must be able to gain *access* to them in order to deliver the needs that you have identified
3. They must be able to *afford* the solutions you have on offer and be willing to pay that price
4. You must be able to meet their needs and generate *profit* for your business

You can establish needs through a process of fact-finding and establishing objectives. This can be achieved through the use of customer surveys and where viable, face to face interactions. How recently they made similar purchases is a good indicator. The more methods you have to gain access to prospects and customers, the more opportunities you have to influence them. You can make worthwhile information available, provide advice and offer buying opportunities. You will be able to gauge to what extent they welcome contact from you and the number of times, if any they contact you. Ensure that all contact is logged and calls to you are returned.

Affordability levels can be assessed by gathering research data based on socio-demographic factors. For larger or ongoing purchases you may wish to conduct credit scoring through one of the various agencies that offer these services. For existing customers you can grade them based on their reliability for settlement of your invoices.

Profitability levels can be established by making comparisons between your best and average customers. For example you could grade your top 20% of customers based on their profitability to your business and make available special offers to them on a regular basis. You can build into your calculation of profit a factor based on the requirement for servicing customers. Those customers that generate a "hassle factor" in terms of their constant demands on your service capability can be accounted for.

Customer loyalty

Customer retention has a major impact on the overall profitability of a business. For example, a 5% reduction in defections can improve profitability by 25% or more. A retention rate of 80% means that, on average, customers remain loyal for 5 years, whereas a rate of 90% pushes the average loyalty up to 10 years. The lifetime value of a customer, who is retained and developed over many years, is many times more profitable than a short-term customer.

Customer retention has a major impact on the overall profitability of a business.

This involves the long-term retention of customers who are having their expectations met or exceeded on an ongoing basis. It is a constant challenge due to increases in customers' expectations over time and competitor activity seeking to gain market share. There is a difference between basic customer satisfaction and ongoing customer loyalty. This is described in the following diagram:

True customer loyalty

Satisfaction starts when customer's basic needs are being met. *Bonding* occurs when the company is acting in the customer's best interest. *Personalisation* is achieved when the company understands and anticipates the customer's needs. *Empowerment* begins when the relationship is on the customer's terms and under control. True *loyalty* is when the company and the customer are fully vested in each other.

Developing trust and commitment
The three dynamics of developing trust in a relationship:

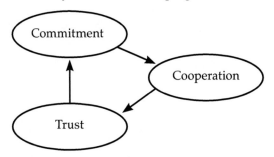

Developing trust and commitment

> *Trust can be established with
> a firm commitment to meet
> customers' ongoing expectations
> through regular cooperation and
> effective communication.*

Trust can be established with a firm commitment to meet customers' ongoing expectations through regular co-operation and effective communication. Understanding customer priorities is a key requirement. For example, matching timescales is important so that projects can be delivered on time and within budget. Keeping customers informed of progress and other worthwhile information demonstrates commitment and helps build trust.

Transactional -v- relationship marketing

Improvements in relationship marketing have come from shifting away from traditional transactional-based interactions with clients. Historically, interactions were typically not coordinated effectively. This was mostly due to keeping the marketing functions, customer service functions and quality of delivery functions all separate.

By having a more customer-focused and integrated approach, the client relationship can be managed better which results in higher client satisfaction. This reduces the much higher costs of customer replacement, compared to customer retention. It requires a long-term view achieving long-term customer loyalty. For example, sending out regular customer newsletters can help build loyalty. This shift is explained in the table below:

Transactional Focus	Relationship Focus
Orientation to single sales	Orientation to customer
Discontinuous customer contact	Continuous customer contact
Focus on product features	Focus on customer value

Transactional Focus	Relationship Focus
Short timescale	Long timescale
Limited emphasis on customer service	High customer service emphasis
Limited commitment to meeting customer expectations	High commitment to meeting customer expectations
Quality is the concern of productions staff	Quality is the concern of all staff

Transactional -v- relationship marketing

Use of guarantees

Guarantees can help to build trust at an early stage. Part of the process of overcoming the initial barrier to entry for new customers is the perceived risk of using a new supplier. This risk can be reversed by the effective use of guarantees, free trials and money-back offers in the event of non-satisfaction.

Customer research and the use of questionnaires

Customer questionnaires can be used to demonstrate the importance of feedback. Valuable feedback can enhance service levels and quality factors by contributing to the refining process. This demonstrates a spirit of co-operation with customers and provides valuable research information on customers' needs and requirements.

Sample questionnaire

The following is a sample survey that can be used to gain greater insight into customer requirements:

Customer Questionnaire

1. What tangible benefits or results have you received by using our products and services?

    ....
    ....

2. Would you be prepared to recommend us to your friends and associates?
    ☐ Yes   ☐ No

3. What additional products, services or solutions would you like to be made available from us?

    ....
    ....

4. How can we improve our products, services and staff to make buying from us a better experience?

    ....
    ....

5. How important to you are the following elements in selecting a supplier?

	Not important	Very Important	Don't Know
Price competitiveness	☐	☐	☐
Quality of service	☐	☐	☐
Technical knowledge	☐	☐	☐
Range of services	☐	☐	☐
Strength of relationship	☐	☐	☐
Delivering results	☐	☐	☐
Market presence	☐	☐	☐
Brand personality	☐	☐	☐
Reliability	☐	☐	☐

6. How would you rate us in these areas?

	Poor	Fair	Good	Excellent	Don't Know
Price competitiveness	☐	☐	☐	☐	☐
Quality of service	☐	☐	☐	☐	☐

Technical knowledge	☐	☐	☐	☐	☐
Range of services	☐	☐	☐	☐	☐
Strength of relationship	☐	☐	☐	☐	☐
Delivering results	☐	☐	☐	☐	☐
Market presence	☐	☐	☐	☐	☐
Brand personality	☐	☐	☐	☐	☐
Reliability	☐	☐	☐	☐	☐

7.   Your name, position and company name

....

....

Thank you for completing this survey.

Providing astonishing customer service

Customers are the lifeblood of any business. How you manage your relationship with customers to find, keep and grow your customer base is an essential element in your business success.

How we manage and meet customer expectations is fundamental to the ongoing wellbeing of our customer relationship. The philosophy we have in maintaining and building our customer relationships determines the quality of that relationship. Key ingredients in the relationship include how well we manage:

• To display a positive attitude
• To enjoy their presence
• To give them a pleasurable experience
• To be caring, thoughtful and present with them

The customer service challenge

It is human nature to look for and expect improvements over time. Constant progress in areas such as technology advancement, speed of travel and improved communication methods builds our expectations as customers. Our customers' expectations of service quality therefore increase over time. The level of service expected today from a customer is likely to be at a greater level than it was when they first became a customer.

---

*The level of service expected
today from a customer is likely
to be at a greater level than it
was when they first became a
customer.*

This is true of business customers as well as personal customers because business customers are a collection of individuals. In order to meet this increasing expectation we need to provide ongoing and constant improvements to our levels of service.

When we initially pitch for business to a potential new customer it is pitched to match our understanding of their expected service levels. When their expectation levels are met and we satisfy their needs they agree to become a new customer.

Over time as our customers' expected service levels increase, our competitors will be pitching to this higher level in order to win their business. If we are still providing the same level of service that we were providing when they first became our customers, then there is a growing gap of expectations. This is the gap between the perceived service levels offered by our competitors and the service levels we are offering. This is when the customer relationship becomes vulnerable and we are likely to lose them to our competitors.

We can list customers according to four key categories of customer loyalty, as follows:

Customer category	Level of customer loyalty
Well serviced customers	Highly loyal
Existing customers	Potentially vulnerable loyalty
New customers	Developing loyalty
Poorly serviced customers	Highly vulnerable loyalty

The customer service challenge

In order to manage this challenge, we need to be constantly striving to improve customer service levels and looking for ways to be more customer-friendly. The following chart illustrates this point:

Customer Perception of Service

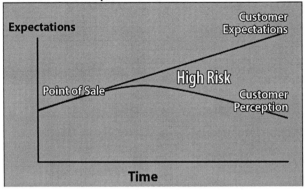

The increasing gap between customer expectation levels and actual delivery

> In order to meet customer's expectations fully, an organisation requires every process and every person to be tuned to support customers' needs.

In order to meet customers' expectations fully, an organisation requires every process and every person to be tuned to support customers' needs. Staff must work together as a team and as "internal customers" of each other to best meet the needs of "external customers". Effective team working and people integration are essential elements. This may require re-thinking about work and colleagues.

You may like to conduct an exercise for groups of staff to consider these key issues as follows:

1. Consider the benefits to you and to the organisation of providing better service to customers
2. What attitude, knowledge and skills would be appropriate for maximising these benefits in the workplace?
3. List the causes that lead to poor levels of service within the workplace

The following is a list of customer service skills and other professional qualities:

- Ability to build warm, friendly relationships based on trust
- Visible concern for and care about people
- Telephone and other communication skills
- Empathy and rapport building qualities
- Commitment to quality
- Ability to think strategically
- Ability to think tactically
- Ability to demonstrate effective customer response
- Ability to recognise good customer service, creative and innovative ideas
- Firm belief in the value of their work
- Enthusiasm, self-confidence and resilience
- Capacity for effective hard work

Having sound product knowledge is also a key requirement. Being able to apply the knowledge appropriately can be used to aid the customer service experience. Focusing on and being able to communicate customer benefits rather than product features will assist initial and ongoing customer satisfaction levels. This includes avoiding the use of jargon and keeping technical explanations as simple as possible. Ultimately customers buy results, solutions to their problems and good feelings. They don't want to be bombarded with technicalities.

Positive motivation for staff
Your staff members have to be motivated towards truly delivering ongoing customer excellence. This includes

factors that build their confidence and feeds their self-esteem. Such factors include an environment of recognised achievement, responsibility, advancement and personal growth.

Performance standards for meeting customer needs

Getting it right the first time can save time being wasted by having to do it again. Promises that are made need to be realistic and kept. People need to take individual ownership of issues to be resolved. Communication needs to be clear, brief and jargon-free. Courtesy has to be shown throughout with both internal and external customers. Good records must be maintained in order for other people to pick up and handle issues part way through. This helps manage absence periods. Customer information needs must be noted and provided.

Communication by telephone

Effective telephone communication is a highly specialised skill. Elements of the message that would be present during face-to-face communication are missing. Without visual messages we are forced to fill in the gaps. This can easily lead to mis-communication and misunderstanding. Various studies have been performed to establish the relative importance of different elements within the communication mix. You may be surprised to learn of the significance of physical and visual elements such as body language. The following table lists the various elements in communicating the message:

Element	Face to face	Voice only
Words	7%	20%
Tone of voice	33%	80%
Body language	60%	0%

Elements of communication

Using voice only, we have to work much harder to communicate the complete message with accuracy and reliability. When dealing with customers, our voice needs to be happy, enthusiastic, confident and clear. For example, spelling names is a good discipline to have. This can eliminate errors where they commonly occur and may cause offence.

Dealing with customer complaints

When customers complain, more than anything else, they want to be heard and understood. One of the most powerful ways to release all that pent up emotion and frustration is to let them have their say and allow their concerns to be acknowledged and recognised. Even the most irate customer will eventually run out of steam and begin to calm down. This is your opportunity to empathise with him or her and to gather information to ensure you fully understand the problem. Active listening skills are essential at this stage.

Asking open questions will allow you to get to the root of the issues. Do not attempt to justify your position, as this will aggravate the situation further. Once the issues are fully understood, you may be able to offer options and suggestions to address the problem. There is likely to be a course of action you can agree with the customer that will satisfy all parties concerned. Take personal responsibility and ensure that the agreed actions are carried out. Remember that, in any confrontational situation, you have individual rights and you don't have to take abuse.

Active listening skills

In order to build rapport with customers it is essential for them to feel that they are being heard and understood. This involves active listening, clarifying and summarising to understand the customer's situation fully and to gain all the relevant facts. This requires an attentive and supportive approach, treating the customer seriously and developing trust.

In order to build rapport with customers,
it is essential for them to feel that they are
being listened to and understood.

It may also be necessary to challenge customers in a non-confrontational manner to encourage them to clarify their objectives and priority levels. It is important to identify the key priorities appropriately to ensure that focus is applied to the correct elements. This is much more likely to lead to the appropriate action.

Your role then becomes one of working with the customer to sift through potential options and weighing up the relative advantages and disadvantages of each option. The resulting action then becomes an agreed solution that is workable from your perspective as well as theirs.

Case Study

A major high street retailer needed to provide best practise and policy information to their workforce. Their existing systems helped the Human Resources (HR) department to respond but, as 80% of the questions were straight policy and procedure queries, the labour cost for providing this service was very high. Leading edge internet based tools were used and now several hundreds of HR questions are resolved by the system—only one HR person is now needed to administer the system for the entire workforce.

Questioning techniques

You will want to use the appropriate technique with customers in order to elicit information and gather the correct facts. Here is a table containing various questioning techniques together with their purpose:

Type of question	Purpose	Example
Closed	A direct question that would normally produce a YES or NO response. This helps to establish facts quickly.	Would delivery next week meet your requirements?
Open	Enables you to explore information more fully. Offers an opportunity to open a discussion and enables concerns to be raised. Would normally start with HOW, WHAT, WHEN or WHERE.	What would you say are your main priorities?
Leading	Directs the conversation down a particular path. Needs to be used with care if you want to focus on the customer's agenda and not yours.	And you would want to avoid all of the ongoing servicing costs wouldn't you?
Hypothetical	Enables ideas and options to be explored in a non threatening way. Allows your thoughts to be tested without confrontation.	How would the offer of an up front discount enable you to extend the contract over one or two years?
Probing	To elicit more information and to challenge ideas. Encourages customer to clarify their thinking.	How would you justify your position on this issue?
Multiple	Several questions that are raised together. Good when used on a rhetorical basis to stimulate ideas. Otherwise needs to be avoided to prevent confusion in the customer's mind.	So you think this is better value than that one? Is it because of the higher capacity? What if we could offer you a variable capacity solution?

Types of questioning techniques

Delivering Powerful Presentations

When you are communicating, either on a one-to-one basis or to groups of people, you will want your message to be clearly understood and acted upon. In order to achieve these objectives, your presentation needs to be planned and delivered with impact. Gathering and organising the appropriate material will enable you to prepare the detailed content of your talk. Using notes appropriately and controlling your nerves are important ingredients towards presenting your message with confidence.

Preparation, preparation, preparation

There is no substitute for making the time available to prepare fully and thoroughly. Be clear about your subject matter and why you are the right person to make the presentation. There are several facts that you will want to be aware of before the appropriate preparation can begin. Where possible, be sure to give yourself plenty of time to prepare. Try to establish in advance where your presentation fits in to any other speakers who are presenting at the event. Ensure that you have an agreed time slot for the duration of your presentation. Decide in advance whether you want to keep some time aside to answer questions from your audience.

There is no substitute for making the time available to prepare fully and thoroughly.

Information regarding your audience will help you to pitch your message appropriately. This includes the likely numbers of people who will be present, their age range, sex and interest group. Visit the venue beforehand, where practical, so you are aware of the size of the room and the layout that will be used for the presentation. You will be able to check the facilities that are available and the requirements for presentation equipment on the day. Consider issues such as how you will be introduced and whether there will be a facilitator or chairperson present.

Developing creative ideas for your presentation

The best designed speech is one where you have created and developed your own ideas that you are able to share with conviction at the event. This will add freshness to your talk and will encourage your audience to be open minded. This enables you to be much more persuasive and win the audience over to your way of thinking. Make sure you fully consider and meet the needs of your audience with your presentation. You are able to develop ideas by starting with your overall theme and jotting down related topics through word association. Here are a number of creative headings to get you started:

- Opposite points
- Outrageous points
- Amusing points
- Witty points
- Beautiful points
- Harmful aspects
- Pleasing thoughts
- Down to earth aspects
- Annoying thoughts
- Luxurious aspects
- Social implications
- Controversial aspects

Creative headings for developing a presentation

Construct your material by first considering the conclusion of your message. This will create a path for you to follow with the preparation of the material. Determine the style that you will be using for the presentation. For example, you may choose a humorous, serious, provocative, controversial or entertaining style. Group your material into a series of main headings and sub-categories. Make sure your ideas are organised into a logical sequence. There are three key stages to the communication of your message. These are:

Stage	Time guide
1. The approach or introduction (*tell'em what you are going to tell'em*)	20%
2. The main body of the speech (*tell'em*)	60%
3. The conclusion or finale (*tell'em what you told'em*)	20%

The three key stages of a presentation

Slot the contents of your message into one of the three key stages and develop links between each stage. Draft out the detailed content in full, checking facts, dates, names, places etc. as you progress. The introduction stage can include a welcome, an outline of the agenda and the main objectives of your presentation. The main body will include all your detailed subject matter. The conclusion can include a brief summary and a call to action.

Always ensure that you make your own notes. Use large enough writing with double spacing to allow you to read them at a distance. Pick out phrases to be emphasised with coloured highlighters. Ensure that you build in pauses that will add impact to key points. By repetitively reviewing your notes you will be able to remember all the key elements.

Every time you are given the opportunity to speak in public, take it.

Controlling nerves

There is no substitute for practise. Every time you are given the opportunity to speak in public take it. This will enable you to practice refining your speaking skills. Good preparation gives you more confidence and helps to control nerves. Nervous tension is caused by fear. Here are the main fears of public speaking:

- Fear of your audience
- Fear of failure
- Fear of the unknown
- Fear of rejection
- Fear of not being heard or being misunderstood
- Fear of stage fright

Being confident in your ability and being passionate about your message will help you to control your nerves. Imagine that everyone in the audience is your friend and wants you to succeed. Consider that this could be your last opportunity to have a significant positive influence over the group of people that you are speaking to. Use natural gestures and don't be afraid to move around. This will add to your confidence and help you get your message across effectively. Avoid unnecessary distractions by ensuring that doors are closed, the lighting is adjusted and curtains drawn to cut out unwanted daylight.

If you are new to public speaking, consider recording your talk in advance. Use the recording to review your performance. Ask a trusted friend or colleague to give you honest feedback. The talk does not have to be word perfect. Just ensure that you communicate the important elements of the message. You can afford to leave out less important elements. Remember, your audience only knows what you actually said rather than every detail that you intended to say. Be yourself and allow your unique personality to shine through.

Consider that this could be your last opportunity to have a significant, positive influence over the group of people to whom you are talking.

The first thirty seconds

Your audience will make judgements about you very quickly, so it is important that you get off to the right start. Take your time moving to your speaking position. Scan your audience left, right and centre and make eye contact, where possible. If you are faced with bright lights you will still be able to make out the outline of your audience and you will appear to be able to make eye contact with them. Let your audience see you settle, appearing relaxed and in control. Take a few deep breaths before you begin to speak. Use a "stand at ease" posture with your legs slightly apart and your knees bent. Display openness with your arms in an unfolded position and preferably with the palms of your hands open and visible. Control your breathing so that it is even and pitch your voice to reach the back of the room. Here are some suggestions to get you started with your opening words:

- State your main theme
- Introduce the audience to itself
- Topical news item or a major issue
- Local interest story
- Personal story (don't be apologetic and use humour appropriately)
- Controversial statement (can work well if you are taking part in a debate)

Adding impact to your message

There are several ways of adding impact to your message by what you say, how you say it and what you do. Moderating your voice by varying the volume and tone combined with the use of pauses will add colour to your message. The use of plosive sounding words such as "boom", "bounce", "power", "press" will add impact. Use simple words and short sentences. Scanning newspapers beforehand for vivid phrases can help you source the appropriate material. Use figures with imagination, for example 1,500 people or three jumbo jet-loads. Use phrases that appeal to the five senses, for example "feeling as smooth as silk". Here is a list of power words:

Impact	Word
Warmest	Friendship
Gentlest	Tranquillity
Most tragic	Death
Saddest	Forgotten
Most revered	Mother
Most bitter	Alone
Most comforting	Faith
Most beautiful	Love
Most cruel	Revenge
Coldest	No

Adding impact to your speech with the use of power words

Case Study

A number of universities and food manufacturers in collaboration wanted to promote courses and careers in food technology and science to six-formers. This required working with the team to develop an integrated strategy to get the appropriate messages to the target audience—teachers and six-form students. The result was an integrated plan with a website, extranet, seminar and printed collateral all being produced. Phase 2 is now under way with a search engine optimisation programme being implemented.

Interview with
Sam Allardyce

What does success mean to Sam Allardyce?
The answer to that is about achieving your own goal and once you have achieved that goal you need to move on to the next one. You can call it a vision or a dream, or an inspirational dream if you like, but to set it and try and achieve it and then if you can achieve it, then that in itself is a magnificent achievement.

You then have to set the next one and determine the realistic goals and the all inspiring dream that you want to aim for. You must not be detracted from setting your own goals and your own dreams or visions. This is probably very limited to a lot of people in life but I have been very fortunate that I have realised some of my dreams.

What qualities are needed to reach the top in football? Is it talent alone?
They are probably spotted as a footballer because of their ability to begin with, but I think that's quite easy to spot and I think beneath that, the biggest thing as to whether you will achieve the top level or not depends on the mental attributes of the person as they grow up and what their own desires, beliefs or dreams are.

Then to really focus and dedicate themselves one hundred percent on the dream and that can then evolve in football in particular to many different things. Now, being the complete athlete is part and parcel of the football world so it is not just about how to control the ball it is about the physical strength and also the mental toughness.

When I say 'mental toughness' that is not from the physical point of view, it is in terms of, is he tough mentally? Does he tackle? Does he put his head in where it hurts? Of course all that is also important as well as making brave decisions at the right time and picking out the right pass. When all those things are put together it makes an exceptionally good footballer. Talent comes further down the list and I think everybody would agree with that.

The amount of pure talent I have seen drift out of the game is phenomenal, purely and simply because some of the other factors were missing. On sheer ability alone you cannot get to the top.

How important is a player's mental attitude then, for instance after an injury?

I think that if there is an inner burning desire to be ultimately successful and an injury comes along, as long as the injury has been treated in the right way (and bearing in mind that in today's society we can fix almost anything), you can recover from that injury and follow your career again. It does sometimes deter somebody's career because mentally they never recover from it, but also in other cases it can be a life changing experience for them.

When they overcome the injury it has mentally made them stronger and, all of a sudden, they realise just how much they would miss football and find they might just have taken it slightly for granted before. This can be an advantage for some people.

Why did you bring in a sports psychologist?

Well I suppose from a number of seminars where people were talking about the mental skills needed in football. I think if you broke down the mental skills, they are far greater than the motor skills, so we went away and worked an awful lot on pace, strength, mobility, agility and fitness techniques, technical ability, passing techniques, heading techniques and control techniques.

If you actually listed the mental attributes needed for a top premium footballer, they are more than twice the motor skills, so I felt it important to move down that route and of course I had an experience in the States that also came back to mind.

The biggest problem was finding the right sports psychologist for our industry. I had to find somebody that could come into the football world. It is extremely difficult for them first and foremost because they are open to a barrage of very complicated athletes who are very sharp and very witty and, if you don't know your stuff, they will be the first to find out. It is a huge task for anybody to come in and attract their attention because, in the main, there is a huge negative response to this to begin with, so meeting up with the company we now use, Advance Performance, at a 7.30am breakfast seminar at the Reebok stadium was rather a difficult task for me because I am a late bird rather than an early bird. So, up at 6.30am to see this breakfast seminar at 7.30am and just getting past the second yawn, all of a sudden this delivery came from the Advance boys, and they just held the whole room together for about an hour and half.

What benefits do a motivational company like Advance Performance offer you?

The organisation side and the mental growth of staff and players is something that is being done more in industry, not just football, and I think that their aspirations to challenge you mentally are very good indeed. They always send you away thinking about yourself first and then how you can become better and more confident and how you can deal with people better. And this is about a people skills thing and I think we all revolve around people in football. This game is about talented players but it is also about managing people and about getting the best out of people. As motivational experts we learn from their experiences, but also these guys will actually bring that down and modify it for you and give you better ideas to take the positives forward, so they actually see your qualities and help you develop and enhance them.

You moved into management, but were sacked at West Brom. What got you through that experience?

That particular time of moving from a player into the coaching fraternity was a huge bonus for me because jobs in football are very few and far between. When you consider there are 92 clubs with about 2,500 professionals in those 92 clubs, then if you talk about 92 clubs having one manager and one coach, there are few jobs available in this industry, so to move into it after finishing at Preston North End was a huge experience for me which is what I wanted.

Unfortunately, being sacked so quickly from that job was a bitter experience for me which always makes you reflect on yourself, but in the end you have to come to the conclusion that, was it really your fault and if it was, why? Were you just at the wrong place at the wrong time? Have they deterred you from pushing on in this career? I then tried other businesses outside football and always struggled because I wasn't an expert in those businesses. I relied on other people too much whilst I continued to try and get back into football and unfortunately those businesses failed. So football was the only thing for me at that particular time because I was most experienced in that. I decided that I needed to do that and would go anywhere to do it. In the end that resulted in my having to go to southern Ireland to be a player manager of Limerick. That was a great learning experience for me as it was a full time player manager job and a manager of people. Irrespective of whether it was amateur or semi-professional or professional, the skills required was to manage players the same as they are at this Premiership level. So I learned an awful lot from that and then got some success when we won the championship there, and I took great pride in that.

How did you build the range of skills needed to be a Premiership manager?

I think that my experience in the life of football is probably 70% of why I am successful. I chose not to just stay at one club in the end but to go to several clubs in different countries across all divisions. I came across numerous different styles of managing and coaching throughout my time. Then having the unpleasantness of being sacked and having to go down to the likes of Limerick where I had to set up again, it was another learning curve and another learning experience that enhances you to do the job. Then to move out into the business world and understand that football is a business, and to acquire the skills so that you can understand how the finances work and how to conduct contract negotiations and stuff like that, is another learning curve that I went through to make myself the best I possibly could be in each individual area, and I think that whole experience has got me to where I am today.

What perhaps is the unique strength that you possess for your job?

I think that it is me as a person. I think that out of all my experiences there is one thing that I will do and that is, I will do it my way. I have to do it my way to sleep and to be satisfied with myself. It's my formula and it probably only works for me because it is unique to me, I suppose. It does not stop me from finding other people as there are some things that they can do better than I can, and for me that is the key to the success that I have had. I understand my strengths and I understand my weaknesses and I try to find somebody that can cover those weaknesses and is stronger than me in that area. I do not take all the credit for what I do by myself; it is about the back room staff that I have built up and the support that for me also brings success.

What is your advice to a retired player wanting to enter management?

I think now if he wants to start thinking about managing and coaching, he should start in his mid to late twenties because there is a certain criteria that is now in place in football that is going to grow and that comes from FIFA and the FA . It is the professional licence to be able to manage or coach set at the highest level which will take you through the whole of the world and Europe with that qualification alone. They should concentrate on that first and foremost and learn all the other skills that go along with it as they gain more and more experience.

Football is changing. What do you think the future will bring, especially for the Premiership?

Well, I think we underestimate our product. We live in a negative environment by the fact that we have a fantastic product in this country that is recognised all over the world as the best league in the world and the most watched league in the world. Sometimes people say it is not the best technically but the bottom line is that everybody in the world wants to watch Premiership football more than any other sport. I think we have a fantastic product and I think that product has been enhanced not only by the introduction of foreign players and coaches, but the development of English coaches and players as well, along with the partnership with Sky TV. I think the two go together well and has produced a fantastic product. I just sincerely hope that we do not press the self destruct button!

llllllllllllllllllllllllllllllllllllllllllllllllllllllllllllllllll

Sam Allardyce was appointed as Bolton Wanderers manager on his 45th birthday in October 1999.

Sam's professionalism and enthusiasm for the game were carried from his playing career which began at Bolton and he is now recognised as one of the best soccer team managers in the UK putting him in prime position for the England manager job in the future.

llllllllllllllllllllllllllllllllllllllllllllllllllllllllllllllllll

Watch this video interview plus many more like it through your free subscription to online business TV portal Expertsonline.tv available to you as a buyer of this book. Just send an e-mail to **info@expertsonline.tv***, including the ISBN number, and the location of where you bought the book to receive your free subscription worth £50.*

Chapter 6

Working as a team

"Remember no one can make you feel inferior without your consent"—Eleanor Roosevelt

Working as part of a team can be a lot of fun. It can also be very frustrating. We want to maximise our contribution to the team and enhance our own skills while doing so. It is right to challenge what we do and how we do it in order to make improvements. This can lead to conflict. By taking personal responsibility for our own actions in a spirit of cooperation helps to break down barriers and build trust. Mutual respect is a key element. By feeling empowered we can all work towards solutions that are right for the team as a whole.

We each have a unique blend of skills, capabilities and talents that need to be respected and protected.

Having common goals is essential to sharing a sense of community. We can help one another through mutual trust. If we are all heading in the same direction, we are more likely to accept help and offer help to others. While we each need to work to our personal strengths, we can take turns tackling the harder tasks. We each have a unique blend of skills, capabilities and talents that need to be respected and protected. By encouraging each other, we can achieve much more and be more productive as a team. We are able to provide mutual support to each other at all times, including times of crisis.

By working together we can have a positive influence on others and we can help ourselves at the same time. How we respond to problems without criticism or blame, dramatically improves harmony within a team environment. We need to take personal responsibility for our part of the problem. It may be that our communication of a task was unclear. We can explain the negative impact that an issue has on us without apportioning blame. Where we are relying on others to carry out delegated tasks, we can ensure that we explain the requirements of the task in detail and repeat explanations when necessary. Being able to express our ongoing confidence in the ability of others helps to build trust.

Here are some of the most important words we can use while working as part of a team:

- 6 most important words: "I admit I made a mistake"
- 5 most important words: "You did a good job"
- 4 most important words: "How can I help?"
- 3 most important words: "Would you mind?"
- 2 most important words: "Thank you"
- 1 most important word: "We"

Dealing with different personality styles

We can improve effective communication by accepting and recognising our own personality style and that of others. We each have an individual style that has a leaning towards certain attributes. Accepting this facet of human nature can help us to understand how we interrelate with others. We are all a highly complex blend of personality traits that combine into a unique individual. We are also constantly changing throughout our lives based on our own experiences and influence from others. It is not about putting people into a box in order to describe their personality style. It is about understanding ourselves better, understanding the behaviour of others and being prepared to adapt our approach to improve effective communication. This is a three-stage process, as follows:

1. Understanding our own personality style
2. Understanding the personality style of the person we are communicating with
3. Adapting our style to improve the quality of the communication

We can begin this process by asking ourselves two questions. This determines our own personality style:

1. Do I have a tendency to be more outgoing or more reserved?
2. Do I tend to be more action-oriented or more people-oriented?

We can improve effective communication by accepting and recognising our own personality style and that of others.

Ask two simple questions

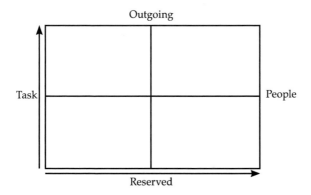

Determining personality style

For example, people who are more outgoing and people-oriented find it naturally easier to be around others. In turn they can often be naturally entertaining, influential and inspiring. Each of the four personality styles have both helpful and unhelpful traits depending on the style of the other people with whom they are communicating.

Here is a summary of typical traits that are exhibited by the four personality styles:

Personality styles	
Direct	Inspirational
Decisive	Interactive
Dominant	Impatient
Defiant	Irrational
Cautious	Sensitive
Critical	Shy
Calculating	Sweet
Corrective	Supportive

Typical traits exhibited by the four personality styles

Once we understand our own personality style, we can gauge the style of the person with whom we are communicating. If we know them reasonably well, we can do this from our knowledge of their personality traits. If in doubt, we can ask them using sensitivity in our approach. People like to talk about themselves. Asking them whether they are naturally more reserved or outgoing and more people-oriented or task-oriented is unlikely to cause offence.

Armed with this information, we are able to work actively on modifying our own style to enhance our communication with them. For example, let's take an extreme case to demonstrate the process. We will assume that we are naturally very reserved and highly people-orientated whilst the other person is extremely outgoing and fiercely action-orientated. In this situation, we can best adapt our style by being more decisive and expressing ourselves clearly and firmly. The other person would respect a no-nonsense approach and would certainly be frustrated by any sign of dithering or uncertainty.

Motivating others to achieve

Any organisation is only as strong as its weakest link. Demanding performance from your people is essential to minimise weak links in your organisation. Ongoing performance management systems are required to track performance. Strengths and development areas need to be identified in order to recognise and reward people appropriately.

Your pay and reward system needs to be aligned with the attitudes, skills and knowledge that you want to encourage in your organisation.

Your pay and reward system needs to be aligned with the attitudes, skills and knowledge that you want to encourage in your organisation. A pay and reward system that is linked to performance is part of this process. There is a direct link between how results are achieved and how people are rewarded. Targets for performance can be set against a number of key performance indicators. Targets can be individually based and team based. The best performance is often achieved when there is recognition and reward for both individual and team based performance. The following lists give examples of typical key performance indicators for different types of roles and responsibilities. They can be combined in order to match the requirements for specialist roles:

Key Performance Indicators

KPIS for leadership roles

- Motivation
- Energy levels
- Self-esteem
- Decision-making
- Ability to focus
- Effective communication
- Vision
- Stature

KPIS for marketing roles

- Marketing research
- Understanding customer value
- Planning and managing campaigns
- Design and production
- Testing and monitoring
- Maximising return

KPIS for sales roles

- Planning and preparation
- Approach and presentation
- Completing profitable business
- Agreeing next actions/ follow up
- Competition/market awareness
- Record keeping
- Managing territory
- Positive attitude

KPIS for support roles

- Personal motivation
- Time management
- Customer focus
- Record keeping
- Technical knowledge
- Effective communication
- Working within a team
- Positive attitude

Recognising positive motivation

We all need motivation to act and that drive comes from within ourselves, based on two opposing forces. These are the needs to obtain gain and to avoid pain. External influence can be applied to motivate others. We each have a range of primary motivation factors that change over time. We act in accordance with these factors. Motivation ebbs and flows within each of us based on our internal thought processes and our external environment. Sustained motivation requires constant "refuelling".

Motivation ebbs and flows within each of us, based on our internal thought processes and our external environment.

The following is a list of the most common positive motivators:

- Achievement
- Recognition
- Responsibility
- Advancement and growth
- Enjoyment
- Support

By focusing on the positive behaviour in others we are able to offer encouragement. We tend to repeat the behaviour that gets noticed. By using punishment as a motivator we are focusing on negative behaviour. Whilst this can work as a short-term motivator it is best avoided for long term motivation in the work place. It is much more effective long term to redirect effort when mistakes occur. This requires us carefully managing our responses to others so that we can avoid being perceived as critical or personal.

When problems occur we need to be able to explain the problem without criticism or blame. Always ensure that any admonishment is given in private. Be specific and focus on behaviour not on personality. We also need to take personal responsibility for our part in the problem by acknowledging this to others. We can explain the negative impact that the problem has on others and ourselves without being critical. We can repeat instructions carefully and in detail to avoid miscommunication. We can express trust and confidence in others ability to complete tasks accurately and to the required standards.

Giving the appropriate praise is a powerful, ongoing, positive motivator. It requires us to look for constant improvement in others even if it is only small. We are able to offer positive encouragement by recognising the improvements that are being made in the performance of others. Giving praise has the best impact when given immediately and when it is related to specific situations. It helps to share our feelings about the positive effect that an improvement has on others and us. Always ensure that praise is awarded in genuine situations. Be honest and sincere. Where possible give praise in public in front of other peer groups of people. This way praise gets noticed, is acknowledged and is shared.

Recognising signs of demotivation

There are many factors that can create dissatisfaction in the work place leading to the demotivation of your people. It is important to manage these elements appropriately and to avoid setting up unnecessary causes for discontent.

Giving appropriate praise is a powerful, ongoing, positive motivator. It requires us to look for constant improvement in others, even if it is only small.

Some of the key elements include the following:
- Interpersonal relations
- Company policy
- General work conditions
- Status and supervision
- Pay and reward systems
- Stability and security

There are a number of stages to becoming seriously demotivated. This state will have a damaging effect on others and has potentially serious consequences for the business as a whole. Being able to recognise early signs of demotivated behaviour are therefore useful management skills. Recognising early signs of demotivation enables you to decide on the most appropriate action. The longer the issues are left without being addressed the more serious they become and the more difficult to resolve.

The following diagram shows four stages of becoming increasingly demotivated:

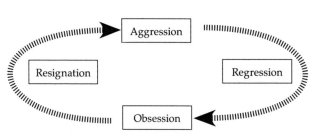

Source: Frederick Hertzberg
Recognising signs of demotivation or stress

Aggression: This takes the form of demonstrating aggressive behaviour towards other staff members or towards the organisation. This is likely to be irrational and out of character.

Regression: The behaviour becomes increasingly petty and childish. This can often be malicious and spiteful.

Obsession: Preoccupation with what may seem like petty or small issues. This is often focused on the root cause of the dissatisfaction.

Resignation: Appearing disinterested and resigned to the situation. This is often combined with extreme cynicism towards others or to the organisation.

There are better ways to manage these issues effectively. For example, one indicator would be to recognise signs of aggressive behaviour in a person who is not normally aggressive. Recognise that the cause of the demotivation or stress may be coming from a source outside the work place. If you know your staff well then they are more likely to share these issues with you and keep you abreast of developments. Whilst conditions of dissatisfaction exist, positive motivation in other areas will have little effect. The source of the dissatisfaction must be removed or corrected to a reasonable extent before positive motivation can begin.

Whilst conditions of dissatisfaction exist, positive motivation in other areas will have little effect.

Recruiting the right staff

Recruitment is always a very time consuming and high-risk activity. It is also an extremely crucial element in building the success of your business. With the right team around you there is no limit to what you can achieve. The ability to have tasks delegated and shared with diligence, sensitivity and effectiveness is a wonderful attribute for a business to have. People work best in a nurturing environment where they are able to learn, grow and enhance their skills. This requires to be achieved at a pace that matches the needs of the individual and the needs of the business. Finding the right people that can work well together is fundamental to this requirement.

The ability to have tasks delegated and shared with diligence, sensitivity and effectiveness is a wonderful attribute for a business to have.

Generally, you will want to employ individuals who are healthy, positive and are good team players. It is recommended that you include both one to one interviewing methods as well as group interviews with several candidates at the same time. For specialist roles, group recruitment centres enable you to assess and compare several candidates together. These centres can be held off site if appropriate, for example at a local hotel. There are numerous types of aptitude and suitability tests. These include verbal reasoning, numerical ability, spatial ability and psychometric testing. As part of your selection and induction process you need to be able to impart your future vision of the business and provide the appropriate initial training programme.

You will want to ensure that your recruitment processes are both robust and compliant. Specialist advice is required to ensure that through the right process and contract of employment you are taking account of essential legal requirements such as anti-discrimination and illegal workers.

From start up to maturity, all businesses require sales personnel and this is one of the most difficult roles to recruit for. You want ambitious individuals and effective communicators. You also want people who are going to fit in with the culture of your business. The most cost effective and lowest risk method of recruiting is to employ people who are known to you or have been recommended from a trusted source. Advertising in local newspapers or trade journals are good ways to obtain candidates in greater volume. Here is a sample advertisement for a field sales role:

EXPERIENCED SALES/
KEY ACCOUNT REPRESENTATIVE

Are you self-motivated and able to achieve results? Do you have a natural sales flair and three or more years experience in the "xyz" industry? If so, you could be right for our team. We are an independent "abc" company supplying a range of "def" products and services to the "ghi trade/industry/market place".

Responsibilities include developing the existing customer base and generating new business from local and key accounts. The position attracts an excellent salary + commission + bonus + car + pension scheme. We provide excellent opportunities within our expanding team for achievers with a positive attitude and enjoy being involved with people.

Please submit your cv to:

Sample advertisement for field sales role

Ideal role profile

For each role you require a profile of attributes and qualities that you are looking for in an ideal candidate. You are then able to match each candidate against this profile to make valid comparisons and select the most suitable candidate. Here is a sample profile for a field sales role in the electrical wholesale market. It can be adapted accordingly:

Candidate Selection Profile for Sales Representative/ Key Accounts

Name of Candidate...

	Criteria	Ideal	Candidate Score (1 to 5)
1.	Qualifications	Academic: A Level Professional: Trained Electrician	
2.	Key Skills	Computer literate Effective communicator Sales skills Presentation skills Planning/Organising Time keeping	
3.	Location	30 minutes from office	
4.	Experience	Sales, 3 or more years Key Account development Electrical	
5.	Driving Licence	Clean, full licence	
6.	Appearance	Smart Professional	
7.	Knowledge	Electrical products Commercial knowledge	
8.	Attitude	Positive Self-motivated Results oriented Good work ethic Ethical & trustworthy Likes people Team player	
9.	Hobbies	Sports/Active	
10.	Financial Standing	Stable	
11.	Fitness/Gen. Health	Top notch	
		TOTAL SCORE:	

Sample profile for a field sales role

Interview with
Eamonn Holmes

What does success mean to Eamonn Holmes?

I suppose I equate success very strongly with survival and not having to worry about paying my bills and taking away the insecurity, and I suppose I harp back to being a child and actively seeing my father worry about paying the bills, really worrying about paying the bills. We all worry about paying bills, but I think back to those days in the sixties when they were in situations where they couldn't pay the bills. That is often the spur and motivation, depending on your background.

My father was an incredibly hard working man and he probably taught me a great business tip in life. He was a carpet fitter but employed by a company and I remember the great debate in the sixties was whether he should go self-employed. This was huge, and I remember as a child watching my mother and father talking about this: 'should I be going on my own' he called it. 'Should I go on my own.' I knew that after that he was in charge of his own destiny. He could determine how long he worked during the day, as he wasn't on a set wage, and I have to say, I then took that tip.

I had a couple of experiences in broadcasting where I wasn't in control of my own destiny and other people were deciding my future for me, and I vowed after that experience had happened to me, where I had trouble paying my bills, paying my tax bills and everything else, that I would remain freelance and not put my eggs in the one basket; and so it remains to this day.

At what age did you decide to become a journalist?

Well ever since the age of eleven I wanted to be a journalist and that was formulated by two things. One was the troubles in Northern Ireland. I was the first of a generation that was very media literate and you would see news reporters on the street corners and then, five or six hours later, you would see the report on the TV, and you would hear the reports on the radio, so people were quite politically aware of what was going on. There was literacy there, in terms of media and politics. The second thing was I was absolutely useless at mathematics. I just had this dyslexia for figures, they would not compute with me. So I was one of two people at my grammar school who would fail at mathematics at 'O' level. You had to have maths to get back for 'A' levels and so, when I was called in by the headmaster of the school to explain why I had not passed mathematics, I basically convinced him that it was part of a plan to be a journalist. I concentrated so much on my English that I had forgotten this exam of mathematics. I always knew that mathematics was going to be a weak point, so being a banker or an accountant was never going to be an option for me. So basically that is why I ended up in journalism.

Everyone has tough times: what carried you through such tough periods?

I am the epitome I think of a company man. I, like most people in companies, love to be loved. We all respond to a bit of praise and a bit of love and a bit of feeling needed. I think in today's corporate world that compassion is very, very lacking.

When it comes down to the pursuit of profit, I am very socialist minded and yet I am quite capitalist minded as well, but I would be very strongly in favour of trade unions and workers' rights and the minimum wage and all that sort of thing. But at the same time I think that you should have a choice and you probably should have the drive to make something separate for yourself.

I found myself wanting to be in the Company, but then the Company dropped me, and I felt this huge feeling of injustice. What was this all about? What really spurs you on is the fact that you have a family and it is not just about feeling sorry for yourself when there are other people depending on you. So feeling sorry for yourself is not an option, and while you have your faculties and you have got your health and some sort of talent and some sort of market ability, get out there and use it.

I do, from that moral point of view, genuinely believe that if you have a gift, whatever that gift is, being good with animals or understanding languages or in my case finding broadcasting relatively simple, you should use it. I think it is doing a dis-service to yourself not to make the most of that gift.

I think a lesson you can apply to whatever your business is, whether you are producing cardboard boxes or whether you are you are a TV presenter, is adaptability and success can be measured in many different ways. Success can be measured by the amount of money you earn, the amount of exposure you have, or if you are quoted on the stock exchange or just by survival and, in my case, as a television presenter, survival is very, very important. So many people go right up and then right down again and they are forgotten after a year or two. I have been doing what I do for 23 years. It's a bit like the grand national—you go over a fence and you say, 'blimey, I'm over another fence, I'm over another fence, I might even win'. You are still there and still on your feet and there are 44 fences to take!

One of the ways of surviving in my business that I've learned is to understand what the market is doing. When I set out, I wanted to be a sports writer, that's what I wanted to be, but my first job was as a farming reporter. I did not know anything about farming. I remember phoning my journalism lecturer and I said, 'Mrs Fitzpatrick I've got a job but the trouble is it is as a farming reporter. I am a City boy born and bred, what do I know about farming?'. And she said, 'Eamonn; rule number one of journalism is to find out'. I have been doing that ever since. So whether it's been about snooker or horse racing or interviewing someone from *Home and Away* (and I have never watched an episode of it in my life) you find out about it.

But therein from wanting to be a sports reporter often your destiny is not in your own hands. The market comes along and says we want you to present a programme on TV about TV programmes and you say, 'I know I can do that. I have not been offered sport so I will do this instead', and then the type of presenter you think you are as in presenting something like GMTV, the market changes.

GMTV has changed over this last ten years. It is not the same news reactive programme it was then. It tends to be much more magazine oriented and lighter in content, so I have changed my presentational style doing this and I am much more of an entertainer maybe than a journalist on this programme. The sports jobs have all dried up because now in sport they only want either ex-sports men or women or girls that are very good looking. Ten years ago the idea of a girl presenting a football programme would have been unthinkable and now everybody accepts it and a lot of these girls are very, very good so I have no difficulty with that. What you have to accept though is that there is not the market for slightly overweight, middle aged men like myself doing sports. So although I was geared to do that along with Des Lynam and whatever, it will now not happen. So what did I do? I said, 'right what can I do?'.

I went out and looked at quiz shows and nobody would give me a job as a quiz show host. They said, 'but you don't do quiz shows, so therefore you can't do them'. I thought, 'well how can I prove this to them?'. So, as a national TV presenter, I went back to Belfast where they offered me a quiz show for very little money and my agent said, 'You are mad. Don't be doing that, it's ridiculous. A complete waste of your time'. And I said, 'No on the contrary, I want to go back there so I can say to people that I do this'. And I did a quiz show which ended up being the top rated quiz show in Ireland called *All Mixed Up* for many years and, as a result, I then spoke to a guy who was working the scoreboard for this programme who was working on the National Lottery programme in Manchester, and they asked if I would do five minutes on the Wednesday night show in Manchester. I finished here at GMTV in the morning and I would do a four hour drive to Manchester, do that programme and do a four hour drive back and get back to London at 4am and do GMTV. But as a result of that five minute programme I was then offered quiz shows: *Playing for Time*, *The Buck Stops Here* and, most important of all, *National Lottery Jetset*, which is the most successful Saturday night lottery show format ever.

I can tell you it was the best thing that ever happened to me and it was simply by learning to be adaptable. I never thought that I would be a game show host, but now I am like Tom O'Connor and *3-2-1* and all that.

In terms of achievement, how important is being honest with yourself?

I say to my children at exam times (for example, to my youngster who is 10 years old and is doing his 11+ which still exists in Northern Ireland and it's a big worry for kids at that age) that as long as you have done your best, not so much even for me, that as long as you can say that to yourself and only you will know if it is a serious situation. We all know when we have done our best, therefore you know how much you have left in the reserve tank.

Why do you think people do not achieve their full potential?

I think that it is a question of confidence, a question of belief, a question of their background, their schooling, their culture, the way their parents treated them, their physical looks. It can be lots and lots of reasons why people do not push themselves and lots of reasons why others do push themselves. Funnily, another motivational factor for me is that I really do not think I am the best broadcaster in the world by *any* means and yet I am kept going in this business which, in many ways, has become superficial because it relies on your looks. Obviously the older you get the less looks you tend to have anyway and however bad I think I am, I look around and this business is full of people who think they are brilliant. They really do and I think however crap I think I am, I am better than him or her, but the difference is, I know my limitations—so many of them don't and I actually find that a great incentive.

It keeps me going and I think that no matter what your job is and when you have your down moments, you must look around at someone who has no sense of their limitation—they just plough on and then I think, well, if they can do it, I can do it.

How important is building up a bank of knowledge and skills?

I do not believe in putting your eggs in one basket. I do think you should acquire knowledge and knowledge is power and information is power and translating that is often what age and experience brings. I don't like the concept in society where you are too old to do a job. Maybe physically you may be too old to do certain jobs but often our best skills, and man management skills particularly, improve the older you get. I know, looking back at my situation in my mid twenties, I was in a terrible hurry, so you might have been brash and you might have been insensitive to other people around you and now I would be in a situation where I've got the experience and I can give advice. I think I am quite good at giving people advice. I think I would be a good manager and I think I would be quite considerate to people around me. At the same time, it is easier to spot a shurker, easier to spot bluffers and I also believe that by and large most people in most walks of life are bluffers.

What is your view of work life balance?

It is a big problem for people and I think it is a big time bomb waiting to explode in this country. We adopt the American ethic of work, which I do not think is necessarily a good thing. They have a different culture, with a different way of leading their life.

Work life balance is very important. When I signed my last contract at GMTV, money was not the main factor because I realised that you can be the richest corpse in the graveyard. As my father used to say, 'there are no pockets in a shroud', and I genuinely went for a deal here whereby I reduced my time as opposed to taking more money that was on offer to me. That did not go down well in terms of the corporate company here. They are mainly interested in your presence but I have responsibilities of a young family. I commute from Belfast, and time is of an essence. I have pass times and I do not want to get into a situation where I look back and say I was not there for my children. I hurt when I am away from my children, and I hurt when I am away from family around me. I don't work as well and I think I work very, very hard at getting a work life balance. It is not easy. I have made it work in my circumstances and I thoroughly enjoy it. But not everybody has that flexibility. One of the ways you can get that flexibility is becoming freelance or running your own company, surrounding yourself with good people.

Are there any books that have helped you along the way or that you have simply enjoyed?

A very good friend of mine is called Bill McFarlane, and we were sports reporters together on BBC Breakfast News at the end of the eighties and into the nineties and I was going through a bad patch at the time. I had just lost a job and Bill and I shared a flat in London together. We were both working very hard. But while I stayed in the media, Bill went on to be a media trainer and a motivational speaker and he has written a book called *Drop the Pink Elephant* which can be found on <www.broadcastingbusiness. com>. His business is called the Broadcasting Business, and in that book he outlines a lot of things in terms of life-work balance and dealing with situations both in business and private life. Often when I feel my batteries are low, I play a round of golf with Bill, and he is very, very good at pepping me up.

The other person I find is a great inspiration, because we all tend to think troubles only exist in our own life, is Alex Ferguson, Manager of Manchester United. I love the idea how he defends his players and how the players will go that extra mile for him and put in that extra tackle. So I like his style of management; it would not work for everyone but it is interesting to know that Ferguson, however much of a god he is to Manchester United supporters, has his own troubles with the corporate side of the business, and he does his own deals. I was reading recently that prior to the 1996 cup final against Liverpool he refused to lead the team out because he was not being paid what he deemed to be his fair bonuses, and the club had to come to an agreement in the tunnel on the day or else it was going to be the Club Secretary or the Chairman who was going to have to lead the team out. I quite like that tactic as there is an element of the trade union bit in that, both in terms of the striking element and in terms of the negotiation, and I genuinely believe in a fair day's pay for a fair day's work and that workers should have their dignity.

The third book I would recommend is something like Clement Moore's *The Night Before Christmas* which is very short or CS Lewis's *The Lion, the Witch and the Wardrobe* to show that there is life out there besides work, there is magic, there is fantasy and that basically at heart we are all children and I like the idea of escapism and that maybe, at the end of the day, work is not the be all and end all.

In years to come how would you like your career to be remembered?

I would like to think people regarded me as being good at my job. Again, my father was a carpet fitter but he always said that if a job is worth doing it is worth doing well and he was a master carpet fitter. He earned absolutely very little money doing what he did and worked very hard for what he got. He took pride in it, and I always remember when I was young I thought, 'well dad you did all that work and you got seven quid for it, why would you bother doing that for seven quid?', and yet he still had the same amount of pride in the job that I would for getting seven thousand pounds for doing the job. I think people in television are obsessed with ratings, and they come to the presenter and say that the ratings were not very good yesterday and I say to them, don't know, don't care because I do the same job whether the ratings are up there or down and do not try and make out that I do it any differently. It may be your fault, it may be their fault or whatever it is, but it is sure as heck not my fault as I do it exactly the same way each day.

||||||||||||||||||||||||||||||||||||||||||||||||||||||||||||||||||||||||||||||

Eamonn Holmes is one of the UK's best known and most successful broadcasters.

Born in 1959 in Belfast, Eamonn established himself as a top broadcaster, fronting a wide range of prime time TV and Radio shows, including the award winning GMTV and Sky News.

||||||||||||||||||||||||||||||||||||||||||||||||||||||||||||||||||||||||||||||

Watch this video interview plus many more like it through your free subscription to online business TV portal Expertsonline.tv available to you as a buyer of this book. Just send an e-mail to **info@expertsonline.tv**, *including the ISBN number, and the location of where you bought the book to receive your free subscription worth £50.*

Chapter 7

Developing customer value

"Everyone who got where he is had to begin where he was."—
Robert Louis Stevenson

Your business offering is unique. Understanding your uniqueness and communicating this to your target market with relentless marketing vigour are some of the keys to achieving greater customer value. You need to know how and why you are different and how you offer greater value to your market.

You need to know how and why you are different and how you offer greater value to your market.

The following list of questions is designed to help you focus on these elements and to consider other ways of creating more value for your business:

1. What are your most important business objectives?
2. What shape does your business need to have (i.e. staff numbers and structure) in order for you to be fully resourced in achieving these objectives?
3. How do you determine the right price for your products and services?
4. What is your exit strategy? Do you have one?
5. To what extent are you working in or on your business?
6. What proportion of your team's potential is currently being realised?
7. How do you demand the best performance from your people?

8. What reward system do you have in place for all of your people based on their performance?

9. How do you ensure that you have the right people in place working to their strengths?

10. What ongoing and regular training do you have for your staff?

11. To what extent are you using direct response marketing methods to promote your business?

12. What process do you have in place for creating up-selling and cross-selling opportunities to your existing customers?

13. How do you maximise customer referral opportunities?

14. How do you make best use of endorsements and testimonial statements?

15. How do you segment your customers appropriately for marketing purposes?

16. To what extent are you using multiple marketing methods to communicate with your target audience?

17. How do you create and develop alliance partnerships with other businesses to share opportunities?

18. What methods are you using to gain free publicity through the use of effective public relations (PR)?

19. What do you know about your competitors' levels of customer service?

20. What information do you have available on your customers retention and attrition rates?

21. What do you really know about your best customers?

22. How do you thank and welcome new customers when they use your products and services for the first time?

23. How do you communicate your unique product or service offering to the market?

24. What processes do you have in place to manage the key risks that your business is exposed to?

Maximising your USP

Many businesses fail to ever fully understand and capitalise on their uniqueness or USP (Unique Selling Proposition). Do you have a clearly understood USP for your business? Do you use it to the full?

Every business, just like individuals, is unique. While you may be working in an extremely competitive market (and most businesses are), your business will have a unique combination of elements that you are able to offer to your market.

Creating a USP

It is well worth spending the time to create the USP for your business. The following steps will help you.

1. Start with a list of the *features* of your product, service offering or treatment
2. Convert the features to customer orientated *benefits*
3. Consider competitive factors in these key areas
   a. Your price competitiveness
   b. Your solution
   c. You as a supplier
   d. Your people
4. Distil the above elements into a list of combined offerings
5. Remove any items that are duplicated by competitors
6. You are left with your USP

An example of a USP using a wholesale supplier
1. Features
- Competitive prices
- Over 4,000 product lines from over 100 manufacturers
- Range constantly reviewed
- Situated in the South East
- Convenient for motorway network
- Convenient for major air terminals
- Convenient for European port routes
- Next day delivery on most orders

2.   **Benefits**
- Plenty of ongoing choice and availability through one source
- Money savings
- Time savings

3.   **Competitive factors**

a.   **Price**
- Able to compete very strongly in some niche areas

b.   **Solution**
- Meeting a wide range of customer needs
- Tailored solutions

c.   **Supplier**
- Established and reliable
- Trustworthy

d.   **People**
- Personal service
- Aspire to be true "Business partners"
- Experienced and knowledgeable
- Speedy and friendly service

4.   **Combined offering**
- Very competitive range
- Tailored solutions
- Reliable and trusted source
- Speedy and efficient
- Personal service
- Shared expertise

5. & 6. USP

A very competitive range of tailored solutions delivered through a reliable and trusted source, offering speedy and efficient, yet personal service and equipped to share expertise. For best effect this needs to be captured in a short meaningful statement. For example, "Always there for you".

Here are some better-known brands USP statements (or slogans) that provide more examples:

Company	USP
Peugeot	The drive of your life
Swatch	Time is what you make it
Dominos Pizza	The pizza delivery experts
Vauxhall	Raising the standard
Durex	Feeling is everything
Nokia	Connecting people
Toyota	The car in front is a Toyota
British Airways	The world's favourite airline

Example USP statements for well known brands

The AIDA formula

When planning campaigns, you need to consider the explicit role of the marketing communication methods and materials being used. There are four key marketing communication roles and an effective formula you can use with each. This is known as the AIDA formula. This is an acronym for:

- Attention
- Interest
- Desire
- Action

Every piece of marketing communication needs clear objectives and expected outcomes. This can be managed using the AIDA formula. The formula is based on the psychological steps people go through when responding to marketing messages.

(A)ttention

In order to create attention to your message, you require a benefit oriented and customer focused *headline*.

(I)nterest
Attention soon wanes unless it is then focused on something of interest. This needs to capture the imagination and be thought provoking.

(D)esire
This involves encapsulating the benefits and feelings of ownership of your solution. This will enable you to create desire for your offering. You want to make people live the experience in advance and leave them wanting more.

(A)ction
Overcoming inertia is the main barrier to action. You want to maximise the perceived benefit of "gains" and avoidance of "pains" to motivate potential buyers. Perceived loss can often be a greater motivator than expectation of benefits.

The AIDA formula needs to be applied to the four key roles you undertake when communicating marketing messages. These are known as DRIP roles:

(D)ifferentiate
Are you looking to differentiate your offering from competitors' offerings?

(R)emind
Do you want to remind people of information they have had previously?

(I)nform
Are you looking to educate and inform people, adding to their knowledge?

(P)ersuade
Do you want to influence and persuade your target audience, changing views or creating actions?

Direct response marketing methods

One common misconception when looking at attracting new customers, is attempting to obtain maximum profit from the first purchase. Intelligent buyers are naturally wary of unfamiliar suppliers. This barrier to entry will prevent them from coming to you unless you help them to reduce the risk of their first purchase. The most effective means of achieving this is through the combination of an irresistible offer, backed by money back guarantees. This loads the risk more towards the supplier rather than the purchaser and becomes a much more attractive and compelling buying proposition.

Many business owners shy away from this approach because they are concerned about being taken advantage of, losing money by discounting and making refunds. In reality this does not happen for those businesses that are focused on providing tangible results for customers with their product or service offering. Businesses that follow an added value approach will be greatly rewarded with future customer loyalty and back-end profitability.

Businesses that follow an added value approach will be greatly rewarded with future customer loyalty and back-end profitability.

Effective "direct response" marketing is a proven method to producing a viable means of profitable business. Direct response messages can be communicated through any media including personal letter, email or targeted advertising.

When communicating your product and service offerings there are four key elements that will impact on your success. These are:
1. Targeting
2. The message
3. The media
4. Timing

For example, *targeting* requires communicating with those individuals or companies that are in the market for your solution and would benefit. It is very easy to confuse prospects with suspects if your targeting is unclear. It is very ineffective to send out "blanket" messages to an audience that have no current use of your solution.

The *message* involves providing something of value to the recipient, not just pure sales hype. The message needs to focus on what tangible benefits and results they will obtain by using your solution. There is likely to be several facets to the use of your solution. When applied appropriately they can produce significantly better results for customers. This is information that a serious prospect or existing customer would want to know. Use an informative and educational approach within all your marketing messages.

Turning to *media*, most people have a preference as to how they receive information. For example, they may prefer telephone contact, email or letter. You need to communicate with people using their preferred method as far as possible. The way to achieve this is by asking for their preferred method and storing it for future use.

Timing is critical when it comes to buying decisions. If you are tuned in to your customers and prospects "schedule of buying" then you can communicate at the most appropriate time. Most people buy in phases of purchases. For example they may decorate their home and have their furniture replaced as well, within a short time frame. You can benefit by approaching them when they are making related purchases. Linking with an alliance partner who offers kindred products or services can be a very effective means of achieving this.

Launching new products and services

The commercial viability of your offering needs to be fully considered when launching new products and services. Research prior to any proposed launch will enable you to gauge whether or not a new offering is capable of delivering customer value and profit. In order to establish this there are processes you can follow that will provide a commercial viability factor.

All too frequently businesses make the mistake of launching new products and services on to the marketplace that were never likely to succeed. This situation can easily be avoided with prudent testing prior to launch. This of course will not guarantee the success of your offering. It will however indicate likely success or failure rates.

If you are tuned into your customers' and prospects' "schedule of buying", then you can communicate at the most appropriate time.

The following elements need to be considered as part of your research:

Target Market

Are you able to identify buyers clearly? This includes the main benefits that are being satisfied with your offering and to what extent people will want to buy it. There may be a specific gap in the market that is being filled by your product. Your offering needs to be capable of providing tangible results for customers. How it improves their lives, adds value in some way or removes existing challenges are key factors that need to be satisfied. You need to be able to gain access to potential buyers. They need to be able to afford your solution and be prepared to pay your price.

Need

You will want to identify clear needs for your offering. How does it create improvements for customers? How does it give them more of what they want? How does it take away challenges that exist for people? Does it save money, time or resources? Does it provide a more satisfactory solution compared to what is currently available elsewhere?

Benefits

Are you able to clearly and precisely explain the benefits of your proposed offering? You need to be able to quantify the level of enrichment or saving that it produces. Be as specific as you can as to how it adds value and produces tangible results for prospective customers

Delivery

How will you deliver the product or service to the customer? How accessible is the customer? What are the costs involved in production and delivery? What means of distribution is required? What scope is there for profitability? What pricing policy will you adopt? Who else will be involved in the production and delivery cycle? Where do you sit in the supply chain?

Unique proposition

You need to be able to identify clear differences between your offering and what already exists on the market. It may be a breakthrough development or new technological advancement. More likely, however, it will be more difficult to set your product or service offering apart from competitors. In this case your uniqueness will be a combination of factors. (See Creating a USP, earlier in this chapter.)

Repeat orders

Regular and repeat ordering capability is essential for your offering to be successful. If your offering is a one-off purchase never to be repeated, then you will need to create a method of offering repeat purchases. You can do this by linking the offering to a related or kindred product or service and making it available on an ongoing basis. You do not necessarily have to be involved in the delivery process of each offering. If preferred, you can work with an alliance partner to share the delivery process and the profits.

For example, an estate agent may believe that they offer a one-off purchase with very little opportunity for repeat purchases. Once they have sold a property it is unlikely that the same customer will move again for several years. By partnering with another business they can provide ongoing buying opportunities and share in the resulting profits. A business that provides property maintenance services could be ideal. For example, garden maintenance services for domestic property purchases. With the estate agent introducing their customer to the provider of maintenance services both businesses can benefit from a share of ongoing profits on an agreed split basis and the customers receive a more comprehensive service.

Combined orders

This is where you combine the purchase of your product or service with a related offering at point of sale. For example, by matching a tie with a shirt you can provide a combined purchase opportunity.

As long as you are increasing your average sales value per transaction, you are increasing your overall profitability.

You can offer the related purchase at a discount price in order to provide an incentive to buy. As long as you are increasing your average sales value per transaction, you are increasing your overall profitability.

Assessing viability

By assigning each of the elements a score you can assess the viability of your proposed offering. This provides a likely success factor for your product or service. It also helps to determine what changes or enhancements you will need to consider as a way of improving viability levels, prior to launch. For example, score each of the elements with a rating from 1 to 5. This ranges from 1 being poor to 5 being excellent. Add up the score to provide an overall rating of viability.

In the following table, a score below 30 is unlikely to be viable. If this is the case, you will need to consider how you can modify, develop of enhance your offering to make it viable. If you are unable to make these enhancements then launching your product or service could be commercial suicide!

Element	Score (1 to 5)
Target market	
Need	
Benefit	
Unique proposition	
Repeat orders	
Combined orders	
OVERALL SCORE	

Product life cycle

Products and services move through stages of growth and decline. This is dependent on both internal and external factors. From an internal perspective newly launched products and services are likely to be promoted with vigour and enthusiasm. More mature products and services are sometimes left to decline. External factors include the general market economy and macro consumer purchasing trends. A typical four-stage product life cycle has the following characteristics:

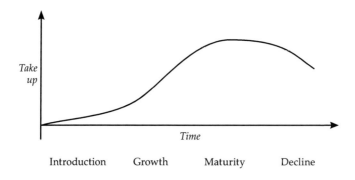

Product life cycle

Winning higher-value sales

In order to win higher-value sales you might like to review and refine your proposal process. A tried and tested method of presenting your offering is more likely to produce better results and higher-value orders. The following is a proposal process that follows a customer-oriented approach:

1. Customer objectives
2. Your recommendations
3. Key features, benefits and deliverables
4. Additional benefits
5. Financial justification
6. Ongoing customer care
7. Testimonial statements and references

Customer objectives

These need to be SMART (Specific, Measurable, Achievable, Realistic and Time-bound). They can be grouped into separate timescales. For example, timescales can be for immediate requirements, short-term, medium-term and longer-term requirements. Base the statements on customer needs. Use motivating words in each objective, such as "improve", "increase", "remove", "gain", "maximise", "expand" etc. State benefits that you know you can achieve for customers.

When customers are looking to buy, they need quality advice from experts who are prepared to share their knowledge and skills as well as provide a solution.

Recommendations

The recommendations are based on your assessment of customer needs and objectives. They need to take full account of your knowledge of the customer and expertise in your market. Ultimately, when customers are looking to buy, they need quality advice from experts, who are prepared to share their knowledge and skills as well as providing a solution by way of a product or service. Recommendations need to be as specific as possible.

Key deliverables

These are more in depth descriptions of your specific product or service offering as applied to the customer's current situation. Where you have longer-term deliverables, then you need to take account of potential changes to your customer's situation and the market place in general. In this case it is worth building in some contingencies so that you will still be able to deliver the best possible solution that is within your control.

Additional benefits

This can include the degree of tailoring that your solution is offering. This ensures that it meets your customer's needs as appropriately as possible. You can also reinforce your ongoing commitment, ensuring that your customer receives value and is able to achieve the expected result from your product or service. Ultimately, it is an enhanced result that people are buying and their satisfaction will be measured by the extent to which this is achieved.

Ultimately, it is an enhanced result that people are buying and their satisfaction will be measured by the extent to which this is achieved.

Financial justification

This includes the price that you are charging for your product or service. Make sure that you include all the separate elements that are included in the price. People do not like unexpected surprises when settling their account. For example, specify all related charges such as delivery, VAT and insurance.

Where possible, relate your price to a tangible result from which the customer will benefit. You can express your price separately as a proportion of a financial gain or saving. For example, "The cost represents 5% of the saving in your energy costs".

Include your payment terms to ensure that there is no misunderstanding regarding when and how payment is expected. Expected timescales for delivery need to be clearly stated. Make sure you are able to deliver within the stated time and within your customer's requirements.

Ongoing customer care

This includes how you plan to maintain customer contact, providing ongoing help, support and advice. If you include a review service, then this needs to be explained fully.

Testimonial statements

These are third-party references from other satisfied customers. Where possible always include the name and the source of the reference. Make sure that you ask permission from the donor of the reference before you use it. Keep original letters and documents available to enable you to validate the reference if required. If a prospective customer would like to contact an existing customer make sure you alert them prior to them receiving contact.

Presenting the proposal

Where possible it is always more effective to present the proposal face-to-face. This is not always viable depending on profitability levels and distances involved. It is always more effective to present the proposal in person if it can be justified in terms of practicability.

Be prepared to review and refine your proposal process to make improvements over time. This can lead to significantly larger sales values and more customers for similar effort. You can use standard proposal templates to systemise the process and save time.

The Concept of Customer Insight Management

A means of having a deeper understanding of customers needs attitudes and behaviours, in order to improve the relationship with them. Rather than just delivering marketing research information, customer insight, requires a contribution to the analysis and strategic use of the information. It is an advanced form of Customer Relationship Management (CRM).

The concept embraces the combination of several sources of available data and competitive information, including marketing research information. It provides the ability to assimilate this information and to be able to be used for the proactive strategic development of the business. Following a data mining process it is possible to apply a range of tools and techniques to gain extensive insight into customer needs.

Specialist internet-based tools enable information to be obtained and tailored with pinpoint accuracy. For example, an electronic magazine can be produced that promotes a range of products or services that are tailored to the individual. Reporting tools report how much time is spent in each section of the e-magazine, thus enabling customers' needs to be identified and met with absolute precision.

The result of such tools facilitates highly targeted "permission" based communications with your target market. This is much more effective than an "intervention" based approach, such as blanket advertising.

Case study

A software company who had developed an intranet for employees to share vital customer knowledge and best practises found that it was not being used because it was too difficult for people to update. Using specialist internet-based tools, a working 76 page intranet was delivered within budget and on time. Any authorised non-technical person is able to update information and, when a change is published, the system automatically tells everyone who needs to know. This system is now widely used throughout the company, greatly improving employee communication and customer insight.

The Benefits of Customer Insight Management

- To enable ready access to combined marketing information of customers needs, attitudes and behaviours
- The ability to continually feed back accurate information from customers, at every point of contact, to improve effective communication with them on an ongoing basis. This process is referred to as "Closed Loop Marketing"
- To maximise orders from enquiries
- To add more relevance to each customer communication
- To improve customer loyalty
- To increase customer referrals
- To increase cross-selling and up-selling opportunities to existing customers
- To reduce customer complaints
- To be able to stimulate greater demand for your products and services
- To assist in designing, segmenting and targeting ongoing offers to customers
- To help develop appropriate and effective marketing strategies

Prospect and customer segmentation

This is the ability to split your data and marketing activities into groups or segments. The key areas for segmentation are:

- Geographic (country, region and town)
- Demographic
- Geo-demographic (combining population and location)

- Personal characteristics (attitudes, motivations, personality style)
- Behaviour towards product (required benefits, usage rate, loyalty)

Data warehouse and data mining

A data warehouse is a purpose-built database extracted from a larger database. Data mining involves extracting data to suit a particular purpose or looking for a particular pattern. Computer based tools enable these processes. Data mining techniques include both Analytical and Predictive techniques.

Case Study

A national wholesale distributor of computer consumable products was concerned about their overall business risk and ability to recover in the event of a disaster occurring. The main issues related to data loss and recovery in the event of fire, flood or burglary. They were looking for an Intranet solution that would be secure and available remotely at any time of the day or night. This was developed over a three month period to plan, design, implement and test their tailored solution.

The result was a system that manages all of their HR, Employment Law and continuity planning processes. This has provided greater business efficiency and reduced exposure to key risks associated with costly, damaging and disruptive events.

Closed loop marketing

Many businesses have numerous data lists spread across different business areas. For example, a customer database, sales database, invoicing database, prospect database etc.

This needs to be combined into a comprehensive marketing database to be used effectively. The marketing database then drives all marketing activities and records all responses. This provides an intelligent source of dynamic information that is being constantly updated and refined. The information contained in the marketing database is used to develop the strategic direction of the business. The information provides access to insights into customer behaviour. One of the challenges of marketing research is to provide accurate feedback of customer preferences and requirements.

Improved customer insight provides information that is behavioural-based rather than opinion-based.

Opinion surveys can often be very misleading. Improved customer insight provides information that is behavioural-based rather than opinion-based. It is therefore much more accurate in enabling more effective marketing decisions to be made, based on reliable conclusions.

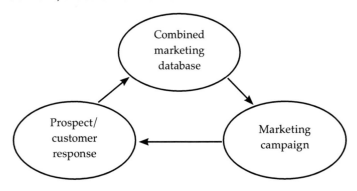

The Closed Loop marketing principle

"Technology is a tool … It needs to respond to, not be expected to change, human nature"—Brian James

Interview with
Nighat Awan

Nighat Awan, what does success mean to you?
Contentment. More than anything else. When you are satisfied with yourself at whatever level, that is success—in my eyes anyway.

How did you build the Shere Khan business and brand?
We were in a different business and I am from a business family, but regarding Shere Khan that goes back 15 years. We were not in the food business, I was in the fashion business but fashion did come in handy even with food. My husband came home one day and said that he had bought this property and he said, 'I am opening a restaurant', and I said, 'hang on a minute, let's take a check here', so he said, 'I am opening a restaurant for fun'. Now remember we were in the clothing trade from manufacturing to wholesaling to fashion and I am thinking my husband wants to open a restaurant for fun!

Little did I know at the time that he had been studying the market for over two years. When he came home at night he had been coming through an area and studying the area and the people. Curry at that time was very devalued, it tended to be eaten with a beer: whereas Chinese was an average of twenty pounds a head, curry was six to seven pounds a head and you had it when you were drunk. He didn't like that; he knew for a fact that people always love a curry. He had done his homework and over the time he had been studying the market, working on planning his staff and finding different people. When he got the opportunity he thought. 'we have nothing to lose, let's just go for it'. Business is a gamble at the end of the day, you can either drop the egg from high up or low down.

It was a massive success fifteen years ago. I was pregnant with my third child and I was very happy in the fashion trade because I had a very good life. I had a brand new outfit every Friday, we had fashion shows and all sorts of other things that went with that life. Very entrepreneurial, as I put it, but it was breeding for me, it was teaching me something and it probably came in the right order, it was fashion before food. Through fashion I learned that I was very artistic in the way that I thought and could put things together, and really that is where it came in handy in the restaurant because I was given the challenge to design it and I did. So I designed it in the very contemporary manner of the eighties, which was all the blues, yellows and plants and all this business, and it was very comfortable and very inviting to go into. So he did it for pocket money but it turned out to be our main business because, from the first day we opened, the doors were busting and the queue never stopped and then, from there, we grew from one restaurant to four, to six, to ten and so on.

What are the characteristics of a successful entrepreneur?

Guts: you have got be able to go out there and deliver and believe in what you do because you have got to sell that on to the next person. So if you believe in something and you have the guts to talk about it, to me that is entrepreneurship. You can go out there and share. I give a lot of talks to women, and they say, 'you are very entrepreneurial' and why they say that is because I am sharing information, explaining to them how they can do it, and becoming approachable. So to me entrepreneurship is about being out there and directly involved with people.

Many people find it hard to grow their business. What is your advice to them?

Well first of all you have to remember one thing; it is not all about you. People make people. You cannot do it on your own, it takes a team of people. If you take the Sainsbury's and Tesco of today they have a team of people underneath them and they have a team of people underneath them, right down to the person stocking the shelves. If those shelves are not stocked, that sale is not going to go through the till. It is as simple as that. So the first thing you have to remember is that you have to believe in the people that you work with and let them grow with you because, by the time you get to the next stage, you need a team of people around you who can take you to that next stage. Where people think that they can do it alone and can have it all is where it all goes wrong.

Are there common mistakes that people make in business?

Yes, very often. First of all they may have put some money in the till and they think it is theirs. They forget that the tax man, the VAT, the bills need paying. This money all belongs to someone else. One of the things that my husband taught me, and my family taught me before that, was that the money that goes in the till does not belong to you, you are only as good as your wage. Anything else needs to go back into the business, because that business will not grow if you do not put the money back in. Any business from the start, you cannot start earning from it immediately. So many business people think that the money in the till all belongs to them. Therefore basic accountancy is very important. So as business people we need to have accountancy knowledge and a certain degree of knowledge in law, we have to have a business mind. There are so many elements we need to know about to become a good business person.

What is your advice about commercial marketing?

Well, marketing and PR are crucial. For example, take Shere Khan: we had a fair amount of luck because we were in the right place at the right time, and luck plays a large part in your life. But it is then about manœuvring that luck, so marketing is important. For example, you have X number of customers coming to your restaurant, how can you market yourself to them? Well, number one, you can do coupons, you can also put information on your tables about the restaurant, you can tell people events that are coming up. We celebrated our tenth anniversary and we made a big hoo haa. Marketing means letting people know what is going on in your business, it is not just letting it stay where it is and a lot of people do not realise this. Once they have opened they think that is it. But that is not enough because everybody else is watching you as well, and you have to be one step ahead, and the only way you can do that is through marketing and PR—and that is what I did.

You mentioned luck, how much does it play a part?

That is a very tricky question. At the end of the day you can take two singers, for example, and they have appeared on *Pop Idol*, and there are three people sat there and they do not like the look of one particular person although she has a fantastic voice, but she does not get through whereas the other person who has also got a good voice gets through because she is exactly how they want her to look. So by the time she has got in front of Simon Cowell, she has won! But the other person who was really, really good does not get through and that is where luck comes in. So to me, luck does play a major part in life, luck is about 80 percent of our life, but it is how we nurture it, and how we take it forward and recognise that we are onto a good thing here. We must work at it now and take it forward. A lot of people do not recognise that.

Are some people born to be entrepreneurs?

Definitely, my brother was a born entrepreneur. He never got through the fifth year at school. He absolutely refused to carry on and today he is worth millions. He is a commercial property dealer. He owns a lot of property around Lancashire. It is his entrepreneurship that takes him forward to sit in a boardroom to talk to people. You have to be able to convince people as an entrepreneur. Take a professional guy for example, and I know quite a few who are very intelligent people with very high IQs—I would not be able to compete with them—but sit them round a table and they have no logic. You sit down with a professor in a room and say, 'right would you like to organise an event?' and they look at you as if to say, 'how would I do that?' and then as you ask them questions, they obviously do not know how to do it. Whereas I could not do their job. I have actually organised a number of events for them and I said what I thought were simple things like, we must do a catalogue, sell spaces in it and they thought it was a great idea. I was thinking, am I losing it here? You cannot blame them though because they have a certain way of thinking as their IQ is very high. So entrepreneurs and business people are very different in everyday life.

Does an enterprise culture really exist in the UK?

Yes I think it is beginning to show. You see it more in young people in everyday life. You didn't see it twenty years ago; people were more shy and sheltered and careful about what they said. Now there is more freedom of speech they say what they feel. It is just about believing in yourself and I think that yes, people definitely are more entrepreneurial, it has been a big change in society.

You have overcome major health problems. What got you through?

I have just had a very bad asthma attack in the last few days and I have been pretty ill, which is why my voice is a bit croaky today. But I rang my younger brother up and I said, 'just tell me, I got cancer from my mother, I have the heart problems of my father, I have asthma from my mother with chest problems, why have I got all this?' and before he could answer I answered my own question, I said, 'no, don't bother, I know, it is because I can take it, God only gives it to those who can take it'. You just have to be positive and move on. I know a lot of people who are worse off than me. I had a motor neurone disease after having cancer and I even remember the date when I collapsed. My daughter was reading the newspaper the other day and someone had this disease. Now I was totally paralysed but I always kept my eye on the ball. This guy in the newspaper went off to Switzerland and gave himself a lethal injection and it was a very sad story as he had very similar symptoms to mine, but my neurologist did tell me that he had two cases side by side, mine and another lady who was the same age and she died. But he only told me this three years later, she died because her attitude was all negative, I survived because I remained positive.

Being positive. Was that a conscious day by day decision?

Yes you have to be. I will give you an example. Someone comes to see you in hospital, you are sat in bed, you are grey, your hair is a mess your arms are dangling and legs dangling on the floor and they will say, 'Nighat, you are not looking very well are you?' and if you say, 'No, I am not feeling well' they will go away then thinking, 'thank God I got out of there'. Alternatively, people can walk into that hospital room and your hair's done and your makeup is done, and your arms and legs are still dropping but you are still smiling and they say, 'gosh you are looking better today' and I will say, 'well actually I am feeling better', because that person has given me that positive vibe. And she will go out thinking, 'I will come back and see her again because it is not off-putting'. So, she doesn't know that I have given her energy and she has given me energy, so it is all about positive energy and you should always be around positive people. My advice to anybody in business is to go where there are positive vibes: where there is negativity, turn around and walk away and that's how I have got through.

Does being positive come naturally to you?

To survive what I have survived there has to be an inner strength within me. When I was told that my tumour was very large on my vocal chords—and I sing—as I was drifting out they said, 'we will not be able to save your voice box'. As I drifted back into normality the first thing I remembered was what they had said but they managed to save my voice box. But what could I have done if they didn't? We would have just had to sort it out; what can you do, that is life? There are a lot more people worse off than me.

Are there any aspirations remaining for you?
Oh yes, I have a lot to do. I work a lot with charities, I work with the Prince's Trust and with business and commerce. I give a lot of talks to people on health and business and I believe I can deliver something back, because I have got the energy to deliver. God has given me that energy to deliver. My aspirations are to become an ambassador of the UN, to become more powerful and then help people in a powerful manner. My dream is to help people through power, and hopefully God will give me that chance one day.

I believe one ambition is to show Western people the real Pakistan?
I give a lot of talks around Burnley, Blackburn and the North West and Yorkshire and when you look around you, the average person looks at TV and sees a certain type of person from Pakistan. When I go to Pakistan, I see a totally different person. Then I think in my heart of hearts, 'surely isn't it only fair that a person born and bred in England but of Asian descent should maybe see Pakistan through my eyes?'. What I see in Pakistan, is the poverty, is the beauty and the cosmopolitan life. It is the seven star hotels and being able to put your hand up and a chauffeur arrives. People do not realise that this is what you can get in Pakistan. I believe therefore that I would love to compare a professional person in Pakistan with a professional person here in the UK including the standard of living they experience. I would love to present that myself on TV and that is my dream as it will also help young people understand.

Are there any books that you would recommend?
Anyone Can Do It by Sahar and Bobby Hashemi. It is about setting up Coffee Republic and is a book I read on

a plane. You know how you start reading a book and you think, 'I have got to keep reading the next page?', well I kept thinking, 'this is me, this is me!'. Their story was very similar to the experience I had with the Shere Khan Group.

My advice to anybody is do not think that you cannot have a dream; you can have a dream, you have to go out and look for it. You have got to find the right people around you to help you realise that dream. A lot of people will say that it is impossible but I read that book about Coffee Republic and that showed that it is possible. You can start with a dream and achieve it.

Another book was by the guy that taught President Clinton in Harvard and it was his advice to entrepreneurs which were things like, you don't need to learn your script, just speak from your heart. This book was exactly as I am and expressed what I feel. I can do that as I have the experience and the knowledge to do it. Books are very important. I am always learning. Knowledge is something that is very important and you can never have enough. I would always say you should read good books if you have the time.

Nighat, have you a final tip for budding entrepreneurs?
My advice which I always give is put yourself in a box and imagine what you really, really want to do and concentrate on that and think right! Don't think you can do everything alone. Then research it and pull all the bits together and then produce a business plan. People say, 'why do you need a business plan?'. In basic business you need to know your maths, you cannot be a business person if you don't know simple maths. You have to know a bit about the law, you need to build these bits of knowledge from everywhere and pull it together and then it becomes logical. You have got to go for it, and if you believe in it enough you will do it. You may not get quite to where you want to be, but even if you get half way that is still further than most.

Nighat Awan OBE is a highly successful entrepreneur and community figure who has overcome a number of personal challenges, and a life-threatening illness, to position the Shere Khan Group as a global brand in the restaurant and food manufacturing market. She has also been appointed chair of the Ethnic Minority Business Forum North West (EMBF NW) set up by the Northwest Regional Development Agency (NWDA).

Watch this video interview plus many more like it through your free subscription to online business TV portal Expertsonline.tv available to you as a buyer of this book. Just send an e-mail to **info@expertsonline.tv**, *including the ISBN number, and the location of where you bought the book to receive your free subscription worth £50.*

Chapter 8

Marketing strategies that produce results

"Whenever you see a successful business, someone once made a courageous decision."—Peter Drucker

Effective marketing communications is playing an increasingly important role in the success of a business. There is a need to justify effective marketing activity. Some of the reasons for the increased activity include media fragmentation, increasing concerns over ethical issues and corporate responsibility, improved customer information and database technology, plus customers who are more demanding and better informed.

Essential to this is an understanding of buying behaviour and the customer decision-making process. The various roles of effective marketing communications, in this context, seek to differentiate, remind, inform and persuade customers towards positive buying decisions. The customer decision-making process is as follows:

1.	Problem recognition
2.	Develop product specification
3.	Information search
4.	Evaluation of alternatives
5.	Select and order
6.	Post purchase evaluation

Buying Decision Making Process

Developing product specifications is an additional step in the decision making process that is typically taken in a business-to-business situation. It is important to consider the decision-making process in relation to the use of various marketing methods. Thorough fact-finding is an essential way of identifying needs and recognising problems that currently exist within the customer's mind.

Thorough fact-finding is an essential way of identifying needs and recognising problems that currently exist in the customer's mind.

Advertising, for example, enables key messages to be communicated that assist with the *information search* process. Product differentiation is essential for *evaluating the alternatives* available in the market. Favourable public relations (PR) can assist greatly at influencing potential buyers. This can be backed by the appropriate use of opinion formers and leaders, to *inform and persuade* potential buyers to *select and order* from your organisation.

During the *post evaluation* process, is important to build credibility and to maximise opportunities for repeat business and referrals to other customers. It is essential therefore that customers believe they obtain the result promised. Ongoing communication through direct mailings of informative and educational materials, can add greatly to this belief. Issuing regular customer newsletters is a good example of this practice.

Selecting your marketing mix

For you to run integrated marketing campaigns you will want to choose an appropriate range of marketing communication methods to promote your offering effectively. This needs to take account of *costs*, degrees of *control*, levels of *credibility* and the ability to *communicate* with impact.

Cost considerations include relative and absolute costs as well as minimising wastage. Control enables you to target appropriately and refine methods as circumstances change.

Gaining credibility from your target audience is essential for your messages to be believed and trusted. You can communicate with impact by personalising your message and interacting with the largest audience possible. This is achieved by selecting the appropriate blend of marketing communication methods. They include advertising, sales promotions, personal selling, public relations and direct marketing. We will consider the use of each method in turn.

Advertising

Advertising can be extremely influential due to its mass media reach through television, radio, newspapers, magazines, billboards and other public display methods. Specific messages can be delivered across different geographic territories and can be particularly effective at creating awareness at the early stages of the product life cycle. New consumer-based products are typically marketed in this way. This creates brand awareness and links the associated product to the brand.

The key limitation with advertising is the inability to measure the impact effectively. Linking and isolating responses to a particular advertising campaign is notoriously difficult. One of the main disadvantages with advertising is the lack of interaction with your target audience. Also, while the costs per contact are low, absolute costs and wastage are high. It is for these reasons that unless you have a large budget or an established brand to maintain, then blanket advertising would be the last activity to consider.

Unless you have a large budget or an established brand to maintain, then blanket advertising would be the last activity to consider.

When considering advertising, the following range of questions will help you to plan an effective campaign:

- What is the role in advertising for this campaign?
- What results are expected?
- Who is the target audience?
- How will you measure responses?
- What key messages need to be communicated?
- What are the compelling reasons to buy the product or service?
- What proposition is on offer?

Sales Promotions

Sales promotions seek to induce immediate sales through some kind of special offer. This requires adding value to your product or service offering to create an appeal to buy now. This is often used to entice customers to buy your brand rather than a competing organisations brand. It can therefore be used as a short-term device to grow your customer base.

One of the main limitations of sales promotions is the inability to delivery a personalised message. There are also very limited opportunities for interaction. One major disadvantage is the immediate loss of profits due to discounting and the use of special deals. Whilst you may encourage new customers to buy your product or service, you will have to work further to establish true customer loyalty. The following list contains a number of sales promotion techniques:

- Money off vouchers
- Buy one get one free (BOGOF)
- Discounts
- Free trials
- Cash back schemes
- Prize draw entries
- Customer loyalty programmes
- Bulk purchases
- Competition codes

Public relations (PR)

Public relations is establishing and maintaining goodwill with employees, customers, suppliers, channel partners and the media. One of the main benefits of good PR is the level of credibility it creates for your brand. It can therefore be useful in creating a positive brand image and generally raising the company's profile. It can be used to communicate a company's ethos, philosophy and values. In times of crisis it can be used to manage poor publicity and damage limitation exercises. Generally PR is available at relatively low cost and can be free in some cases.

One of the main benefits of good PR is the level of credibility it creates for your brand.

Typical PR techniques include:
- Issuing press releases
- Press and public events
- Media relations
- Publications
- Lobbying
- Internal PR (to employees)

Direct marketing

This is an interactive means of gaining a direct response through the use of one or more types of media. This is an excellent tool for highly targeted campaigns and is one of the most rapidly evolving areas of marketing. Growth in direct marketing has mostly been led by increased competition, better-informed customers, increasing costs of advertising and developments in technology. Sophisticated database management tools, electronic point of sale (EPOS) systems and improved communication methods have encouraged activity in this area.

Direct marketing had its roots in mail order; however it has now moved far beyond a "junk mail" approach to a permission-based interchange with prospects and customers through email, the internet, phone, fax and SMS text messaging, as well as traditional post. In addition to the immediate fulfilment of orders from enquiries, it has become an effective method of generating qualified sales leads. Direct response advertising has also become increasing popular. This is where completing a return coupon, visiting a web site, 'phoning or faxing back an enquiry, provides for an immediate response from an advertisement.

Direct marketing has given rise to the new art of database and relationship management through the use of geo-demographic and lifestyle profiling methods. It is now used extensively in both the business to consumer (b2c) and business to business (b2b) markets. Some of the main advantages of this method include market segmentation (targeting), personalised messaging and improved response rates from campaigns.

Personal selling

This is face-to-face selling undertaken by individuals. It is the most influential form of interaction with customers; however it is also likely to be the most expensive element of the marketing mix. This is due to the highly labour-intensive nature of the personal selling role. The higher costs need to be justified with the appropriate higher average value transaction and profitability levels. In some cases this leads to an account management role where particular responsibility is given to handle the most valued customers.

The main aspects of the personal selling role include:

- Prospecting (gathering information to generate sales leads)
- Selling (influencing prospects to buy)
- Market research (gathering competitor and customer intelligence)
- Servicing (maintaining ongoing customer service)

- Customer relationship management (building and sustaining ongoing long term profitable customer relationships)

Managing your marketing mix

It is important to have clearly defined objectives in order to effectively manage a co-ordinated marketing approach. By combining all of the methods appropriately you can optimise your success and profitability levels.

It is important to have clearly defined objectives to effectively manage a coordinated marketing approach.

The relative advantages and disadvantages of various marketing methods are listed below:

Method	Advantages and disadvantages
Advertising	Large reach v high absolute cost
Sales promotions	Individual targeting v low interaction
Public relations	Builds credibility at low cost -v- impersonal/ lack of control
Direct marketing	High interaction v limited reach
Personal selling	Highly personalised v high cost

Advantages and disadvantages of various marketing methods

TripleM™ Marketing (Multiple Marketing Methods)

Why TripleM™ Marketing? If you require maximising your marketing success, you need to consider ways of increasing the return and profitability of your marketing activities.

Adding to your customer base and creating more value from your existing customers is critical. This is a process of finding, keeping and growing customers.

The TripleM™ formula works on the basis of an ongoing process of communicating to your target market. This is a process of informing, educating and nurturing prospects and customers.

For developing new customers, you need to recognise the difference between a "suspect" and a "prospect". Only market to profiled prospects not suspects. It is a waste of time and resources marketing to those who are not identified as clearly within your target market. (Refer to managing customer relationships in Chapter 5).

How the TripleM™ formula works

Typically, many businesses operate with a single dimensional approach to marketing. They may promote product and service offerings through Field sales or telemarketing or advertising or mailings (including emailing). Unfortunately, many businesses fail to capitalise on the incredible power of combining multiple methods. Most businesses take one or two marketing methods and use a scatter gun approach to promoting multiple offerings to multiple prospects (or, worse still, suspects).

Single marketing method

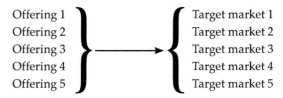

Typical approach using a single marketing method

The smarter and more effective approach is as follows:
1. Take one product or service offering at a time

2. Become laser-like focused on identifying the target market
3. Use multiple methods to communicate with them
4. Keep communicating with them on a regular and ongoing basis
5. Only communicate worthwhile information and valuable offers (avoid pure sales hype)

Multiple methods

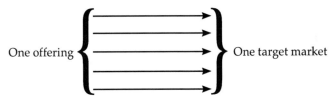

One offering ⎰ ⎱ One target market

TripleM™ Approach

Range of marketing methods

Having selected your offering and target market, the next stage is to furiously market to them through multiple methods. For example, the methods might include:

- Field sales
- Telemarketing
- Targeted advertising
- Trade shows
- Seminars
- Newsletters
- Copy press releases

- Free reports
- Audio or video tapes/CDs/DVDs
- Direct mail
- Tele / video conferences
- Referrals and networking
- Retail outlets

Issue offers that genuinely add value by educating and nurturing your prospects and existing customers.

This becomes part of an ongoing process. So, you might start with a letter to your initial targeted prospect and/or customer list. This would then be followed by say a telemarketing approach with a specific offer. Space out your communications at regular intervals, monthly, usually works well. You then cycle through a range of nurturing steps. There could be a dozen or more of these steps, it's up to you to decide the most appropriate methods for your business. At each stage you are tracking enquiries and following up as necessary. Each stage is bringing the prospect or customer closer to their next buying decision. Typically, 80% of enquiries will become orders within a year. They will buy from you because you have communicated regularly with helpful information and worthwhile offers. You may produce a newsletter that they can request. Always avoid pure sales hype in your offerings. Issue offers that genuinely add value by educating and nurturing your prospects and existing customers.

TripleM™ marketing in action

A typical process for a retail bookstore might operate something like this: the owner would like to promote a range of gardening books at the end of a season to provide shelf space for a new range. The average customer purchase is say £20 per order. So any order over £20 is increasing the profitability of the business.

Step 1: Create prospect and customer database capturing their details on visits to the store. Offer an incentive to provide contact details, if necessary, with a free prize draw

Step 2: Issue an offer to those who have expressed an interest in books on gardening. This could be say a selection of books valued at £50 for £39.97 (assuming this is still profitable based on your direct sales costs)

Step 3: Form an alliance partnership with a local garden centre. Offer them a share of profits on sales from joint marketing campaigns

Step 3: Follow up the enquiries with a telemarketing campaign. Offer a free invitation to an exclusive event at the garden centre. At the event provide information and tips on managing your garden better. Provide drinks and nibbles. The garden centre has an opportunity to market their products. The bookstore has an opportunity to set up a bookstand offering gardening related books and materials. Have a local gardening expert speak on overcoming the biggest hurdles of garden care. Record the expert's talk and include audience questions and expert's answers.

Step 4: Issue a direct mail campaign offering the tape of recording and transcript

Step 5: Issue press release of newsworthy developments linked to gardening readership

Step 6: Issue e-newsletter from web site with an offer of free book voucher to spend in store for every referred customer who spends more than £20

Step 7: Book a stand at garden show. Send exclusive offers to those who come and visit your stand at the show.

Step 1	Step 2	Step 3	Step 4	Step 5	Step 6	Step 7
Create & maintain Data-base	Form alliance partner-ship	Tele-marketing campaign for exclusive event.	Direct mail campaign	Press release	Issue e-News-letter	Trade show

Typical process for a co-ordinated campaign

TripleM™ case study

A well established distributor, marketing IT hardware and software solutions, required to increase its profitable turnover, due to squeeze on margins from suppliers. Existing customer base of several hundred had been developed over nine years. Historically the

Business had been marketing its offerings exclusively through telemarketing and faxed offers to retail suppliers throughout the UK.

The telemarketing process continued with refinements. The refinements included categorising customers, introducing a staff member of the month awards scheme and a programme of skills based training. Over a period of one year, the business started to apply TripleM™ marketing methods. This included the following range of additional activities.

- Direct mail offers
- Alliance partnership offers
- Existing customer feedback survey
- Development of e-commerce site
- Creation of customer loyalty programme
- Attendance at trade shows
- Customer referral offers
- Production of a range of promotional flyers
  Within 18 months, profitable turnover had doubled.

A more effective route to market

By applying the TripleM™ marketing philosophies you can create an infinitely more effective route to market for your products, services and treatments. Keep operating the successful methods you are using, with refinement. In addition start to apply the multiple marketing methods. This involves taking a specific offering to a highly targeted customer/potential customer base. This is highly focused and efficient and produces much higher response rates. Manage costs by expanding the range of marketing methods over time. Minimise inefficient marketing by avoiding a scatter gun approach and lack of targeting, as this is very costly and wasteful.

Immediate Response Methods

All your marketing activities need to be aligned to specific offerings. Every letter, flyer, email, phone call, meeting or approach, requires an objective to *make a specific offer available*.

All your marketing activities need to be aligned to specific offerings.

Give your customers and potential customers, every opportunity to respond in the most convenient way for them. Always provide full contact details with your offers, to include addresses, telephone numbers, fax numbers, email addresses and web site addresses. Individuals and companies have preferred ways of communicating with their suppliers. Make it easy for them to contact you, not difficult.

You then need to apply "immediate response" methods to maximise the return from each offering.

How to produce immediate response materials

1. Create a headline which is customer focused, powerful and benefit-oriented
2. Start the body of your marketing communication with more detail about the promises made in the Headline and details of your offer
3. State clearly the benefits your customers will receive
4. Use testimonials or third-party endorsements to back-up the claims made in your offer
5. Explain what your customers will lose if they do not take up your offer
6. Restate the key aspects and benefits in a closing statement
7. Include a call for action with a deadline date
8. Add a PS after your signature encapsulating the action required and the benefits available

Creating a Headline

The headline of any piece of marketing is always the most crucial element. This includes the opening words in all spoken and written statements. For all communication methods, including letters, faxes, emails, flyers, telephone conversations or meetings—the opening words are critical to success!

---

*The headline of any piece of
marketing is always the most
crucial element.*

Up to 80% of the "influencing power" of any communication is determined by the opening statement or headline. Experimenting with different headlines for each offering can produce incredible differences in response rates. I have witnessed up to hundreds of percent differences by just changing the headline statement in a particular offer. Be as specific as you can, stating values where possible. The following headline produced a 20% response within 48 hours:

> ## "At last ... a reliable, efficient and competitive supplier who recognises and rewards your loyalty."

The details of your offer and customer benefits

Back up the claims made in your headline statement with more detail of your offer. It is important to make your offer as believable and tangible as possible. Make sure it is laden with customer benefits and is totally customer focused. Here is an example of a headline statement followed by details of the offer:

> # Now you can relax knowing that your automated security systems are not likely to break down in the middle of the night
>
> It is now possible to have your automated gates, barriers and related security systems fully maintained and serviced on a regular basis to minimise breakdowns (excluding alarm systems). Speedy response is also available just in case of system failure. We can have your premises secure again with the minimum of fuss, expense and delay. This can be achieved through a comprehensive maintenance programme with a straightforward payment facility.
>
> ## What we will provide for you
>
> We will provide a comprehensive maintenance and servicing agreement for all your automated security systems and associated control equipment. Just in case of any system failure, we also provide a fast call-out service to enable your security to be up and running again without delay. This gives you ongoing peace of mind *in the knowledge that your security systems are truly secure and operational at all times.*

Using testimonial statements

It is important to back up your claims with testimonial and third-party statements from existing satisfied customers. These are easily obtained. You just need to ask. If you have produced a quality result for a customer, they will invariably be very happy to provide a referral statement. Check that they are happy to be quoted in promotional materials. Make sure you always quote the source of any testimonial used.

The power of perceived pain

Human nature is such that we are often driven more by the consequences of loss, than gain. By including both the benefits of gain and the pain of loss, within your marketing messages, you create a powerful motivational force.

By including both the benefits of gain and the pain of loss within your marketing messages, you create a powerful motivational force.

Due to their impact, statements of potential loss need to be managed with care. You want to avoid using scaremongering tactics. All statements used, need to be able to be substantiated and require to be as factual as possible. Good quality research of your market is essential. Here are some examples of loss statements that have been used to good effect:

How much time is left to make a successful claim?

We are concerned that there is limited time left to present a case and make a valid claim. If this opportunity is lost, you will be prevented forever from recovering the money that is rightfully yours. We do not want you to take this risk and this is why we are urging you to take action now. Indeed, over 3 years ago, the Court of Appeal indicated that ratepayers should now proceed without delay, or risk the possibility of running out of time.

It's not worth taking the risk of avoiding regular inspections

You don't have to take the risk of failing to meet Health & Safety requirements and potentially unlimited fines. You don't have to take the risk of being left without service for extended periods. You don't have to suffer from unreliable service and agreed deadlines being missed for work carried out. You can avoid any unnecessary costs associated with the electrical contract work that needs to be done.

Take away the worry of security breakdown

You may have invested very heavily in sophisticated systems to protect your premises from unwelcome visitors. Why take the risk of leaving your systems unprotected. Regular maintenance and service support is vital to maintaining the integrity of your security. This can be a real worry when it leaves you feeling vulnerable and open to security risk. We are able to remove this worry from you by providing a comprehensive "security blanket" to cover all your systems and associated devices. Regular maintenance can also significantly extend the life of your equipment and keep it in good working order. This will minimise replacement costs and the associated hassle of having replacements installed.

Closing statements

Closing statements are used to summarise the offer. They need to be succinct in order to encapsulate the key aspects of the offer. They also need to be completely customer and benefit oriented, to maximise the influencing effect of the call to action statements that follow.

Some examples of closing statements:

You can benefit from our "free draw" with first prize of a top of the range, XYZ solution for your office or home valued at over £1,500. There are numerous other prizes waiting for the lucky winners. So come along, visit our stand, take part in our draw and be enlightened by our amazing XYZ solution. Once you've seen it – you'll just have to have it! It's secure, robust, flexible, powerful, safe, space spacing, economic and environmentally friendly. Come and visit us and discover what incredible offers we are bundling together to provide you with the XYZ plus plus...

To summarise, you have a superb opportunity to attend our workshop and be educated by specialists about the crucial requirements for Health

& Safety, new Employment Law essentials and numerous business development strategies. You will be able to apply these principles immediately to create a substantial and speedy boost to your business. We very much hope to see you there.

The offer in a nutshell

We are able to offer you superb money making and cost saving opportunities with our exclusive range of XYZ products. These are all backed up by a rock solid guarantee of satisfaction. The products are very reliable and of a high standard. In addition, we will reward you with loyalty points for using us. These points can be exchanged for worthwhile gifts at any time. **As an added incentive, your first XYZ order given in February and March will qualify for double bonus points.** Don't delay; act now to place your order and receive double loyalty points.

To summarise, you are invited to a Workshop that will provide at least 100 ideas to grow your business successfully through "Effective Business Planning". You will go away with a documented plan that you can start work on straight away. This will give you total focus and clarity in relation to how you need to drive your business forward. But hurry, spaces are limited to 50 attendees on a first come, first served basis. **You need to respond by Monday 4th August. If you are one of the first 10 to respond, you will receive a free transcript of a recent talk by Brian James entitled "Maximising Business Growth".**

Call for action

Following the *closing statements* in your communication, you need to provide a call for action. Surprisingly, this is an often overlooked step and is typically missing from many marketing communications. You need to state clearly what you expect to happen next and what actions are required from the respondent. Do not assume that the requirements for action are automatically understood. They need to be spelt out with clear instructions in order to generate the maximum response. People suffer from inertia and will not take action unless they are clearly led through the process.

Some examples of call for action statements

How to take up our offer
Just complete our enclosed response form and return in the prepaid envelope provided, to ABC Ltd. Hurry, we are only looking to take on a limited number of new contracts. Return the response form now, so as not to be disappointed. If you respond by 15th April, we will provide a complete and detailed design of your system, absolutely free.
Just complete the form and return without delay. We will contact you as soon as we receive your completed details.

If you would like further information, please telephone: 123 456 7890.

Complete and return the enquiry form without delay.
Remember, this is a genuine free offer and will create big demand. The offer is only available for a limited period. You must respond by 31st July to qualify for our free offer. Therefore, respond today, to avoid disappointment.

Please complete the enclosed confirmation form and return in the prepaid envelope provided or fax back to 000 111 2222. If you would like to speak to us first, please **telephone 000 111 3333**. We look forward to hearing from you and to securing your entitlement.

Add a PS

Interestingly, people will often read post-script (PS) statements before reading the main body of the communication. If the offer has been carefully targeted to the appropriate audience and there is genuine interest in the value of your offer, you may get responses purely through a combination of an action oriented PS and a powerful opening headline. Often busy decision makers will scan through the body of the offer, just to reaffirm a decision they have already made to respond to your offer. Good PS statements are therefore highly influential in gaining maximum response.

Add them after your signature, name and title. Ensure they are action oriented and benefit laden

Some examples of PS and multiple PS statements follow:

PS Your entitlement is waiting to be claimed, without any risk to you. Just send back the completed agreement and we will do the rest.

PS Just complete the enclosed response form. Return the form with your cheque to give you immediate maintenance cover for your automated security systems

PS Just place your order now from the extensive range of XYZ printer toner cartridges. We will dispatch your order without delay and reward you with double loyalty points in February and March, as part of our Loyalty Programme. Don't delay; make the call now!

PS. Your free electrical inspection is available to you now. Respond by 31st July to qualify. Your request will be dealt with on a first come—first served basis, so return the completed enquiry form today.

PPS This is a genuine, no strings attached offer. You have nothing to lose by responding immediately. You will benefit from peace of mind in the knowledge that your business premises are safe from major electrical hazard.

PS Come and learn the essential requirements for maximising profitable growth in your business while minimising the key risk factors. Attend our workshop on Thursday 10th April from 8.30am at The ABC Hotel, Any town.
PPS Amazing value at only £47 plus VAT with no risk, money back guarantee.

PPPS Attendance fee will be credited back to you if you decide to continue on with The Brian James Group Business Development Programme after the workshop.

Everything is a test (how to minimise risk)

Most businesses will allocate funds for marketing purposes. Every pound spent needs to justify itself in relation to the return on that investment. All your marketing activities need to be able to stand independently as individual profit centres. If a marketing activity is not able to prove it's worthiness by way of contributing to profitable business, then don't do it.

How do know what activities are going to contribute most to your bottom line? The only true measure is for each activity to prove itself by way of deliverable profit for your business. You can only establish this through a closely monitored process of refinement. The only true measure of effectiveness is what proves to be effective through the results you achieve. This is where sometimes marketing research can fail (although marketing research does have its place). It has been stated, "The only true measurement is through the court of last resort". This means it is only that which proves to deliver results to customers that can be the only true and reliable measure of what is successful.

In order to establish effective and profitable campaigns, the only consistently reliable route is through a relentless process of testing, tracking and refining.

The value of testing

In order to establish effective and profitable campaigns, the only consistently reliable route is through a relentless process of testing, tracking and refining. This becomes an ongoing process. Even some of the most successful campaigns can always be improved upon. And some previously successful campaigns can sometimes flop due to an unusual set of circumstances. So treat everything as a test.

In order to track effectively, you need to tag and measure every element of your marketing activities. This can be achieved by coding your marketing materials, including all your advertisements, flyers, offer letters, telephone campaigns, field activities etc. Every response or enquiry is then matched against the relevant code. You are then able to measure the effective response of each marketing activity independently.

The real value of testing is that you can start with relatively small numbers and build up, as the results prove profitable. This way you are able to minimise costs and risk to your business.

An ideal number for testing purposes is 5,000. This is a statistically large enough number to provide a reliably consistent result. This doesn't mean that any other number is invalid. You can perform an equally worthwhile test with a few dozen issues of your marketing piece. What you will find, however, is that small numbers will produce a wider variety of response rates. So it is more difficult to decipher what is working and what isn't. Once you find a marketing piece that produces profitable results for your business (at any level), then you can gradually increase numbers. For example, you can go from 1,000 to 2,000 to 5,000 to 10,000 to 25,000 etc. The thing to avoid is jumping from a small sample size to a much larger sample size, in one step. Use manageable increases and measure response rates at each stage. Only increase numbers while the current campaign proves to be profitable. Remember, all marketing activity is a test.

Gaining referrals from existing customers

Unless you are a start-up business, you will have an existing customer base of some size. A large and loyal customer base is an extremely valuable asset of your business. If you are not using a constant and systematic means of generating referrals from existing customers then you are losing out on 50% to 200% of extra business.

In most cases happy customers will provide natural referrals to you automatically. It is human nature to want to share a worthwhile and gratifying experience with friends and colleagues. However, if you are not asking for referrals and offering incentives where appropriate then you are missing out on a greater potential for profitable business.

You can offer a simple gift to your existing customers, such as a discount on future purchases or a gift voucher. This makes perfect sense as you are saving your normal costs of acquiring new customers, which is typically four to nine times as expensive as retaining existing ones. Communicate with your existing customers regularly through a limited offer to recommend a friend or a colleague.

Creating profitable alliances

One of the most powerful ways of growing your business exponentially is by creating marketing partnership links with other businesses. This is the best area to focus on first in developing your marketing mix of activities.

Your existing customer base represents your most valuable business asset. Your customers need to be nurtured, treasured and developed, in order to receive the maximum return from them. You first have to give maximum value to them through your product, service or treatment offering.

Your existing customer base represents your most valuable business asset.

One way of achieving this is by being aware of your uniqueness (your business "reason for being") and sharing this with your customers.

You are able to expand your offering to your customers in two ways:

1. To deliver a wider range of products or services yourself

2. To link with other businesses to offer products or services that they deliver

By linking with other businesses and offering a complimentary product or service to your customers, you are able to share in the profit stream generated. Equally, by linking with other businesses to extend your offering to their existing customer base, opens up a wealth of new customer acquisition opportunities for you.

How a marketing partnership works

From either your existing customer base, or from your business contacts, you link with another business. That business needs to offer a complementary range of products and services. For example, if you run a law firm, you might want to link with an accountancy firm.

You agree to market each other's customer base jointly, by offering:
1. Their products or services to your customers
2. Your products or services to their customers

This needs to be managed from campaign to campaign, so neither business is locked into an ongoing commitment. You agree to split the gross margin resulting from sales generated from the campaign. Gross margin refers to the sales value, less the direct costs of the marketing activity. For example, if it were a telemarketing campaign, you would deduct the costs of the telephone calls. You would not normally deduct staff costs (other than performance bonuses linked to a campaign) as these are part of your overall operating expenses. The split of gross margin needs to take account of which business is delivering the product or service. The "delivering" business would retain the larger share—75%/25% generally works well.

You may agree to continue sharing the profitability for a period beyond the immediate campaign that generates the sale. Some flexibility is desirable. You need to ensure that a clear understanding exists between both parties, of how much is being shared and for how long. It is recommended that this is documented in either an exchange of letters or, alternatively, a more formal referral agreement. (Sample wordings available free of charge upon request to The Brian James Group.)

Case studies of marketing partnerships

A hairdresser linked with six host businesses to make an offer to their clients and staff. The host businesses were big local companies employing large numbers of staff. Within nine weeks the hairdresser had received a twenty two percent response and three months advance bookings.

A manufacturer and distributor of IT integrated solutions (formed in 2002) linked with a European catalogue distributor. A new category was created within the catalogue to market the product specifically. During the first half of 2003, orders placed were in excess of £2M.

A legal services firm provided a range of packaged mortgage conveyance services for Solicitors throughout the UK. This is a highly competitive market and at the time there were over 200 firms in UK that were competing for this business. The business linked with four separate companies who offer land search facilities. Collectively they marketed their combined services. For the legal services firm this doubled their profitable turnover within the year.

A health food shop operated with one retail outlet offering health food products. The owners were looking to expand by opening more stores and wanted to gain a presence in other nearby towns. They linked with the owner of a freehold shop who was intending to close down his business. The two businesses came to an agreement where they spent three months capturing customer information, as no previous records had been kept. This produced a database of over five thousand contacts. A direct marketing approach was then systematically used to promote a range of offers. Within twelve months, this resulted in an increase of gross profit by £100k that was split 75/25 between them.

Exhibiting at trade shows

Taking a stand at a trade show or exhibition can be a very effective means of attracting new-targeted prospects to your business. Preparation before the show and diligent follow up after the show are crucial elements of success. Ensure that you participate only in the shows that offer streams of potential new customers that are in your market to buy. It is a waste of time and money attending events that are either poorly supported or attract the wrong kind of delegates for your type of business. For example if you market office furniture, then a good show to attend would be aimed at facilities managers. You want delegates that are likely to be in your market and have the authority to buy. If possible, attend the show venue beforehand to gauge the best position to have your stand located. An ideal location is near where the refreshments stand is located, as this will attract a constant flow of people past your stand.

Taking a stand at a trade show or exhibition can be a very effective means of attracting new, targeted prospects to your business.

Three to four weeks before the event, send out targeted invitations to prospective attendees. The show organisers can usually provide lists of likely attendees. You can also advertise in the appropriate trade magazines with tested messages that have proven to produce a response in the past. As with all marketing, make sure that your invitation letter is laden with benefits about your product or service offering to maximise responses. For example, provide an attractive offer that is only available by attending the show. This would also be a good time to issue press releases to trade publications and to write articles that get reproduced in issue that are released just prior to the show date.

Arrange your stand with benefit-oriented displays. Greet people in the aisles with the offer of a free entry prize draw that they can participate in by coming to your stand. You can have your people dress in an appropriate theme to ensure they get noticed. It is also worthwhile to participate in seminar and workshop activity. This is your opportunity to impart knowledge to delegates about your product or service. Invite them to attend your stand to enter the prize draw. Offer prizes that are relevant to your business to ensure that you only attract targeted prospects. For example, a business providing courier services might offer a free collection and delivery up to a certain weight and distance.

Once delegates arrive at your stand make sure they are made to feel welcome with comfortable seating and refreshments. Keep them involved by offering product demonstrations and samples where possible. Hand out free reports and other valuable information to educate and inform them about your product or service. Make available special offers that are available exclusively to show attendees.

Most importantly, make sure you gather full contact details from as many targeted delegates as possible. After the show, follow up immediately and relentlessly to maximise your return.

Here is a sample invitation letter used at an education show. It could be adapted for other types of shows:

Dear …

You are invited to join us at the "XYZ" Show

You have an opportunity to come and see the unique *"product or service"* on *"date"* at *"location"* and take part in our free draw. You could be the lucky winner of *"free prize"* worth *"£000"*. This is a prestigious event and location where you will be able to gain lots of ideas and meet many new worthwhile contacts. You will be able to:

- See all the latest innovations
- Gain knowledge to help make the most appropriate buying decisions
- Meet more worthwhile contacts

- Test-drive specific areas of interest (including the amazing *"product or service"*)

The award winning *"product or service"* will be there for you to experience first-hand. You will be able to determine how our *"Your USP"* solution, would be tailored to meet your specific needs. Come and see what educators, business leaders and professionals are all talking about.

Why risk making uninformed purchases when you can gain all relevant information at one event? How else will you keep up to date with latest trends, capabilities and developments in the ever-changing world of education? Don't miss out on meeting key influencers, to help you with your decision making for purchases. Where else can you trial and sample so many product and service offerings under one roof?

Register now

Come along and visit us on Stand *"AA"* to increase your awareness and develop new contacts to improve the quality of your buying decisions.

Register now by visiting www.register.com or by returning the registration form.

Yours sincerely,

A N Other

PS Gain a complete perspective on your needs and buying decisions. Register now to join us at the Show on date. See for yourself the amazing *"product or service"*. If you are unable to make this date, please check our show schedule for other events.

PPS Remember don't miss out on your chance to win a free *"free prize"* Register now and come and see us on our stand. Visit our web site at "www."

Interview with
Anita Roddick

What does success mean to you?

Can I redefine it? I will tell you what I don't think it is. I don't think it's about power. I don't think it's about image. I do not think it's about celebrity, and I do not, not, not, not think it's about the accumulation of wealth. So for my redefinition, I'd have to add that it's transitory.

What was defined as success in the early days of The Body Shop was much different than what it is now. Then, it was about earning enough money to live. That was 300 pounds a week, because Gordon my husband had disappeared for two years riding a horse across South America and I thought, 'I've got all these ideas, what can I do with them?'. I just need to take 300 pounds a week but by the end of the Saturday I didn't take 300 pounds a week!

I remember I had these large baskets in The Body Shop and I put all the products in them and I just knocked on doors and tried to sell them, because I was obsessed with earning the 300 pounds a week. Then, a decade plus later, it was really about being the bravest. I didn't want to be the biggest, I wanted to be brave. I wanted to see if my language of a kinder, gentler way of doing business, which was really just copying what the Quakers had done two centuries before. Now it's about being more of a social enterprise than a financial enterprise, and I think it's about being heard.

If you're heard, your opinion matters , so I guess all defined and mushed in together, success for me is about the freedom to be spontaneous and the freedom to do what you think is the right thing. I think I would have slit my wrists if I had ever thought we'd end up being part of corporate America or England, and the word 'brand' wasn't even floating around when I started 30 odd years ago.

All I wanted was an honorable enterprise. I never even wanted a business, because for me business was seen as a small version of a large corporation and I didn't like hierarchy. Women entrepreneurs hate hierarchy. They try tearing it apart at every given moment. So no, I never thought it would be as big as it was. I knew my idea, whatever I was going to do, was going to be iconoclastic and different and I'd be putting two fingers up at the system, whatever the system was. But no, I would have been fearful if somebody had said to me 30 years ago, 'in, 30 years time you're going to have 250 shops. You're going to be in 55 markets, you're going to be fighting to go into China, you're going to be about to go into Russia'. No way; I mean, because it was fraudulent! Once I had the loan from the bank I was away, which was 4,000 pounds from the miserable bank manager. Bank managers can be just the worst thing for businesses because they protect money, they don't have this entrepreneurial ability to see the idea, and the power of an idea.

It would have been too frightening for me, it wasn't what I was. I was an activist, I am an activist; it was bringing my social activistism into the work place. That's all I wanted to do, and have fun. If I wasn't having fun it wasn't worth doing. I really believe that.

What challenges do you think female entrepreneurs face today?

I think there are some things that have changed since back then: one is that there's now a title called 'Female Entrepreneurs'; two there are great prizes for being a successful female entrepreneur. But still I don't think it's gone far enough.

You can look at this in many ways, you see business schools for example. Very rarely, even in the most established business schools, have they got any courses on Women in Management? Women manage in an entirely different way. It's much more instinctive, much more about networking, much more about feelings. And they're still having to spend ten times more time with their kids than their male partner does. It's still harder for women to raise money for a business enterprise than it is for buying a new car, so that hasn't changed!

And still bank managers are where you tend to have to go for finance as they are one of the very few avenues of raising capital for an idea. So I don't think we've got an enterprise economy that says, 'hey that's a brilliant idea'. I don't think we realise that some of the best ideas are social entrepreneurship ideas. Women live longer, they're healthier in many ways, they live a decade longer in England. They reinvent themselves and women's characteristics, I think, are not better than men's, but equally important in terms of ethics of care and justice. I think they are really important for how we do business in the future, and it seems really stupid that many men will not hire a person just because they're wearing a bra, because they think they're going to leave and have kids. I know millions of men that will leave a business not because they're having kids, but because they just choose to.

So I think it can be hard and what makes it harder for people like myself is we end up being tokens. They say look at that Anita Roddick from The Body Shop, she did it! With no damn help from the government, let me tell you. No help from the system, no help from formal networking or the International Chamber of Commerce. It was about grassroots thinking, and it was about finding your place in the community. I have to say, sadly, I don't think too much has improved.

The Body Shop really came about as a livelihood. I needed to have a livelihood to look after my two kids when my husband went for two years riding a horse across South America. Women are very good at having ideas and mixing what they're interested in and what they're talented at and making some sort of livelihood from it. I was a teacher. I had worked for the United Nations, International Labour Office and I had travelled. That was real for me, wherever I travelled I was usually in arenas, not of western-type civilization, but in areas where indigenous people were. I lived a lot of the time in West Africa, South Africa and on the Indian and Pacific Ocean Islands, and everywhere I travelled I tended to live in fishing communities where I picked up the rituals of the body. Women are good at that; men are lousy at it!

Women are interested in what other women are putting on their bodies. I became a sort of closet anthropologist. Then, when I came back from the travelling ten years later, in my early 30s, I decided to start The Body Shop and it was only going to tread water for two years, and then we were going off to open a pineapple plantation.

Finally got the money from the miserable bank manager who didn't give it to me actually, probably because I was wearing a Bob Dylan T-shirt, and jeans, and I had my two kids destroying his office. Bank managers don't like enthusiasm, so I was going, 'I've got this great idea, and it's going to be called The Body Shop, and I have all these ingredients from wise women around the world'. Well the guy, I think, thought I was going to open up Brighton's first sex shop or something, so he didn't give me the money!

So Gordon, my husband came back to the bank with me and I wanted to look like a man, so I wore my pinstripe suit and we had a plastic folder and a profit and loss thing. We didn't really know what we were doing and he gave Gordon the 4,000 pounds, not me. Gordon handed me the money and he went off to do his trip, and I opened up this little shop in Brighton.

First day I was in trouble because my shop was between two funeral parlors, and they didn't like the coffins passing my shop with the words 'Body Shop' over the top, so they told me to close the shop and to change the name from The Body Shop, which I couldn't do because I had just spent several hundred pounds doing gold leaf lettering which nobody could see anyway. Then I did something very smart, I did an anonymous phone call to the local newspapers saying I was being intimidated by Mafia undertakers, and my husband had just deserted me, so, I knew how to talk to people.

We started with 25 products. It was useless, about as big as a coffee table, so what I did was (and this is what entrepreneurial thinking is all about) I did 5 sizes of everything so it looked like there were 100 products; smart eh?

Hand-written labels not so smart, because the writing ran in the bathroom when they got wet. And so we survived, but we had stories, every product had a story. How I made it, what mistakes I made, don't worry about the black bits they are the dirty footprints of the bees, just scoop it out, you know, lovely anecdotes, anecdotes that adhere to the mind.

Gordon came back and I had opened up a second shop and he sort of came up with this idea about franchising it. It was so funny. We didn't even know the word 'franchising' existed and my friends were saying, 'you can do this'. So we painted the shop green. It was the only colour that covered the damp patches, now it's the colour of the environment!

We sold the idea to friends and then we got a bit more professional and set up a franchise system.

It was so hokey pokey, I can't tell you, but what was really brilliant about it was the community element. We were learning from the Quakers, we were learning from the community movement, cooperative movement, we were learning from the Amish, we were so excited about setting up a community for the development of the human spirit within the workplace, not just a product, and we were a very strong communications company. So we grew but the real reality, if the truth be known, is we weren't a product lead company at all: we had a great product, thank God, otherwise we'd have closed down as it was about campaigning for human rights, that was all we were interested in doing.

We branched out and had over 150 shops and then we made the biggest mistake we ever made when we went onto the Stock Market. Useless, don't ever do it! We did it for a good reason as we wanted to control our manufacturing and have the money to build the manufacturing plant, and to control our recycling, so it was good, but we're suddenly being measured not by how many jobs we were creating, which was our heartbeat, it was about how much you were worth, and that changed everything.

In the end it was very fascistic. I mean the fascism in the City is about very unimaginative bottom line profit and loss, which does not include human rights, or social justice, or environmental protection or any of that stuff. So trying to change the world, the language of business, which we'd started to do really early on in the 90s, was phenomenal, but it didn't stay unfortunately, because the system changed and we all lost the plot in the progressive business movement. We didn't see what was going on. We're all just saying, 'aren't we great?'. We were sharing best practices, but we weren't keeping an eye on who controlled the system.

|||||||||||||||||||||||||||||||||||||||||||||||||||||||||||||||||||||||

Dame Anita Roddick is the founder of the 'Body Shop' chain which now operates world-wide and is today one of the most widely recognised and respected brands in the world.

Through her expertise and insight as a highly successful business woman she helps businesses to prosper in the global marketplace.

Today the Body Shop chain operates in 52 countries and has over 2010 shops. Anita Roddick fulfilled both prerequisites for starting a successful business—she had an original idea and she believed in it.

||||||||||||||||||||||||||||||||||||||||||||||||||||||||||||||||||||||||

Watch this video interview plus many more like it through your free subscription to online business TV portal Expertsonline.tv available to you as a buyer of this book. Just send an e-mail to **info@expertsonline.tv**, *including the ISBN number, and the location of where you bought the book to receive your free subscription worth £50.*

Bonus Chapters

I am delighted to include a number of bonus chapters taken from interviews with a very special group of additional contributors. Each individual is a leading specialist expert in their field with decades of experience and knowledge to share in their chosen subject. I would like to express my personal thanks to each of them by adding their own uniqueness and additional value to the book. Having worked with each of them, I can wholeheartedly endorse their professionalism and expertise. I do hope you enjoy the extra dimensions that each of them adds to reinforce the essential elements that make for business success.

Brian James

Bonus Chapter 1

Corporate Social Responsibility
*by **Catherine Carthy***

Introduction

In order for your business to grow and attract the right employees and customers, it is essential that you manage the expectations of all your stakeholders. Maintaining high ethical standards in your business dealings effects your growth and needs to be considered carefully. In this chapter I am going to look at Corporate Social Responsibility (CSR) and various ethical issues that can effect your business. I will ask you to do a quick organisational assessment to see how socially responsible you think you are.

I will point out the benefits of having clear ethical standards in place and will highlight examples of good practice. I will also give examples of how unethical practices have had an adverse effect on reputation and ultimately the profitability of many organisations. I will provide guidelines on how to set up CSR standards and get training and support so you can implement these standards and bring increased profits to your business.

In the past decade there has been a growing trend towards greater demands being made of organisations by their stakeholders. Consumers expect private and public sector organisations to be more ethical in their trading policies and business dealings. Board directors are being asked to consider the wider impact of awarding themselves large pay rises when their employees receive less than the rate of inflation. Journalists are asked to look at the issue of privacy invasion. It has become more difficult for businesses to ignore ethics because of the risk to their reputation and increasing external pressures to display good practice.

> *'Three things matter in business: reputation, reputation, reputation'.* Simon Caulkin, 1998

What is Corporate Social Responsibility

Corporate Social Responsibility encompasses all the ways in which your organisation and its activities interact with society, balancing the right to trade freely with the duty to act responsibly. It is about the way you meet your wider obligations both to employees and to the wider community. It is about how you contribute to economic development while improving the quality of life of your workforce and their families as well as the local community and society at large.

It's not just about making money but also how you do it. It is a strategic issue because it requires you to examine why you are in business, what you need to do to stay in business and manage the growing expectations of your stakeholders. Adele Kimber writing in Personnel Today (2003) says, *'Corporate Social Responsibility is about meeting the needs of today without compromising the needs of future generations. The idea is that a business has a duty to its wider community – beyond staying within the law and satisfying stakeholders.'*

The European Commission's Green Paper on CSR defines it as 'a concept whereby companies decide voluntarily to contribute to a better society and a cleaner environment'. The Department of Trade and Industry, DTI, says that a responsible organisation

- recognizes that its activities have a wider impact on the society in which it operates
- in response, takes account of the economic, social, environmental and human rights impacts of its activities across the world

- seeks to achieve benefits by working in partnership with other groups and organisations.

Self-Assessment

It will be helpful to do a quick self-assessment on your organisation at the start to see how you measure on a CSR scale.

Unethical behaviour		Corporate social responsibility

It is useful to look at Unethical Behaviour (UB) and Corporate Social Responsibility (CSR) as two opposite ends of a continuum with 0 at the centre. CSR is at the positive end from 1–10 and UB is at the negative end also from 1-10. Where would you put your organisation on this scale?

- How well do you keep your promises to customers and suppliers?
- How do you contribute to the community you operate in?
- What are the ethical practices of your suppliers like?
- How well do you treat your employees, are they proud to work for you?
- What are your Health & Safety practices and procedures like? Do you provide a safe and attractive work environment for your staff?
- What are you doing for the environment, do you encourage recycling, using sustainable energy?
- Are your accounting practices and financial dealings impeccable?

This is just a quick self- assessment so you can start to evaluate your own organisation as we work through the chapter. Many organisations use external trainers or consultants to carry out a thorough assessment, often using focus groups, interviews or surveys. We will provide guidelines at the end of the chapter to help you set us a CSR programme internally. But first we will look at examples of good and bad practice.

The Quaker Influence

Although the basic concepts have been around since the likes of Cadbury introduced housing and education for their workers in the nineteenth century , there has been a re-emergence of the principles in recent years. In the light of specific controversies like Brent Spar and Shell, many companies have developed social and ethical reporting to evaluate and demonstrate their social impacts and to minimize any negative social and environmental effects.

In the nineteenth century the Quakers founded many successful companies such as Cadbury, Friends Provident, Boots and Rowntree and remained true to their social responsibilities. They built villages, towns, communities and schools for their major stakeholders, their employees. The founder of the shoe retailer, Clarks, began as a Quaker cobbler in Somerset in 1825 and the company still manages to keep the Quaker conscience alive. Clark family representatives still sit on the board and continue to ask questions about employment practices, health and safety and employee share-ownership.

The Quakers say they are stewards of wealth and they have a traditional Quaker dislike of redundancy. In twelve years the company has shut down two-thirds of its UK manufacturing while reducing employees by less than 10%. When concern arose about exploitations of workers by a Taiwanese supplier, a delegation of senior managers went to investigate and resolved the issue. In situations involving overseas suppliers there is always a balanced decision to be made about labour standards.

More recent examples

The Body Shop has launched a campaign to end sweatshop abuse and get maternity rights for young mothers in the garment industry in Bangladesh. They are targeting companies in Europe and the USA and asking them to sign a pledge stating that any woman sewing their garments will be guaranteed maternity leave with pay.

The Levi Strauss company closed its facilities in China to protest against the lack of progress on individual freedoms for its workers.

The Environment

The Body Shop is also known for pioneering corporate concern for the environment and in 1991 they phased out the use of PVC from its packaging and products. The head of business ethics, Nicky Amos, said 'Whilst the company acknowledges the versatility of PVC as a packaging and product material, our concern about the social and environmental implications associated with PVC overrides any decision to use it in our products, packaging or shop fits.' The Body Shop provides many more examples to prove that a business can thrive whilst being fair to the people on whom its prosperity depends.

Example from smaller business

For many organisations the community is global and the challenge is great. Smaller organisations can find opportunities more locally and apply them either individually or in partnership with other companies. Chris Moon (2001) gives an example of how Mark Wilkinson, chairman of a privately owned wood furniture manufacturer, applies his firm's ethical approach.

'For every customer order we plant a tree. We choose sustainable raw materials only. We generate links with local schools, taking parties with primary school children. We keep the local post office going by not using a franking machine. If we used a franking machine the village post office would lose our business and if it closed local people would lose too. We do civic jobs in the community church. We're not playing in a vacuum, we're playing it with everybody else in our community. They're all part of the game so the benefits should come to all involved in the game.'

The European Commission has launched a major Pan-European Campaign to raise awareness about CSR among small to medium sized businesses. Europe has 25m SME's and they are the most important driver of economic growth and employment representing 98% of European business.

The impact of unethical behaviour

A responsible organisation recognizes that its activities have an impact on the society in which it operates. It is not the same as compliance with minimum legal standards. The collapse of Enron and evidence of other corporate misbehaviour has stimulated interest in how companies should behave. There has been a serious loss of trust and confidence in organisations as a result of these high-profile cases. Many believe that the well-publicized scandals revealed a pattern of deception by a large number of companies rather than being isolated incidents.

George Moody-Stuart, in Moon & Bonny (2001) has studied corruption on a global scale and has found that it takes many forms and can be intensely damaging. In countries with a lot of corruption less of their GDP goes into investment and they have lower growth rates. They also invest less in education, thereby reducing their human capital, and they attract less foreign investment.

Much has been written about the impact on Nestlé and the consumer boycott of its products in the 1970s when it was discovered that the marketing of its formula milk persuaded Third World mothers to switch from breast feeding. This allegedly led to a high rate of infant mortalities.

British Airways lost more that the £610,000 in libel damages paid to Richard Branson over the 'Dirty Tricks' affair in its underhand campaign to persuade Virgin customers to switch to BA. A few years later, Richard Branson's reputation was challenged again in Virgin's bid for the National Lottery. GTECH refused to provide the technical support he needed and Guy Snowden tried to bribe him to withdraw his bid. In his autobiography Branson (1998) writes:

'In the court case that ensued the jury found in my favour against Guy Snowden and GTECH *and my reputation was restored. In his summing-up, the late George Carman* QC *pointed out to the court that, above any commercial success one might enjoy, one's reputation for honesty is the most important thing.'*

The Importance of Trust

While the costs of being unethical in business are significant and can damage the bottom line, there can also be a significant loss of trust that is difficult to repair. Successful business relationships are built on the conviction that each party believes that what the other person is saying is true. The loss of one's good name comes from a lack of trust. Research has shown that unhappy consumers tell more people about bad service than they do about good service. A company with a previously good name can quickly become infamous for double-dealing, not keeping their promises, treating their employees badly and using shoddy business practices.

'Corruption can undo everything else we are trying to do.'
Dr Norman Borlaug,
Nobel Prize winner

Within an organisation itself a breach of trust has many consequences –

- lack of confidentiality
- less effective teamwork
- lack of commitment
- less loyalty
- resignation of valuable employees

Employees in companies that have been criticised for a lack of social responsibility are often treated negatively. For example, after Brent Spar, Shell employees who had been used to being treated respectfully in their communities found themselves being blamed for their company's mistakes and even their children at school were taunted in the playground.

How managers deal with mistakes made by themselves or others sets the tone for the rest of the organisation and is a key factor in building trust. When energy is focused on covering up mistakes it saps performance, innovation and creativity. Managers may be afraid of disclosing their mistakes for fear of appearing weak, but the opposite is usually the case: admitting mistakes can go a long way towards rebuilding trust with employees.

> *'Without trust, there is no*
> *risk-taking and no innovation.'*
> Patricia Buhler

Leadership expert John Maxwell (1998) likens trust to having change in your pocket. Each time you make a good leadership decision it puts more change in your pocket. Each time you make a poor one, you have to pay out some of your change to your people or your community. Every leader has a certain amount of change in his or her pocket at the start. From then on, he or she either builds up this change or pays it out. When he or she runs out of change, credibility is lost with the team. If, on the other hand, the leader has built up a lot of change through the good decisions he or she has made and then makes a big blunder, he or she can still have change left over and will be able to restore credibility with the team.

The cost of recovery

The effort required for a company to redeem its good name can be enormous. Litigation is costly as well as in and out of court settlements. Then there is the public relations costs to regain public confidence and trust. Someone has used the analogy 'It is difficult to drive full speed ahead with your eyes on the rear-view mirror'. An organisation dealing with the burden of public awareness of their practices will find it hard to focus on the road ahead with its missions and objectives and will tend to use up more energy being reactive rather than proactive.

Benefits of ethical behaviour

While it is easy to find examples of unethical behaviour by individuals or groups which have seriously affected the reputation of a business, it is harder to prove that ethical behaviour will boost business performance. However, research from the Institute of Business Ethics (IBE), *Does Business Ethics Pay?* makes a convincing financial case. It showed that organisations which had a clear commitment to ethical conduct, out-performed those that did not and they were consistently more admired by their peers.

Ethical companies tended to be less volatile which could make them a more secure long-term investment. In terms of return on capital employed ethical companies were clearly superior performers. It was also found that an organisation with a culture of trust and high ethical standards was able to delegate decisions further down the management chain and thereby save on bureaucracy.

Reputation, or the goodwill of all stakeholders, is a significant intangible asset and potential damage to reputation is a key risk that organisations need to manage.

Each year Fortune magazine publishes a list of the 100 best companies to work for in the USA. These companies are very responsive to employees' needs, have a lower turnover of staff and attract more applicants than their competitors 'Employer brand' is the pitch employers make to attract and retain employees. Increasingly talented people will invest their energy and talent only in organisations with values and beliefs that match their own.

> *'Markets work well when fair-*
> *dealing businesses are in open*
> *and vigorous competition with*
> *each other for custom.'*
> The Office of Fair Trading

Research by Axiom Software into graduate recruitment identified that 75% of graduates would not work for a company with a poor ethical record (*Personnel Today, 2002*). In order to achieve this match, managers need to build cultures, compensation and benefit packages, and career paths that reflect and foster certain shared values and beliefs.

In 1999 a survey of FTSE 350 companies carried out by Andersen in collaboration with the London Business School examined how organisations were tackling ethical issues and how effective their actions were proving to be. The use of business ethics programmes had increased significantly over the previous three years and the main reasons identified for introducing them were:

- the desire to protect or improve reputation
- adherence to corporate governance guidelines
- increased emphasis on values and the importance of values in guiding organisational behaviour

Many chief executives tend to see corporate social responsibility as a public relations issue. However, others see that it is on the boundary of PR and HR. Suppliers, employees and customers are all more likely to choose to do business with a company which conducts its operations on an ethical basis. The way it treats its employees and its practices on diversity, employee representation and development will contribute to the picture of a company that is willing to accept its wider responsibilities. In order to motivate and retain employees, employers have to treat them properly. The key benefits of corporate social responsibility for organisations are employee motivation and retention as well as an enhanced reputation in the wider business community.

'Reputation is often an entry point for becoming interested in social responsibility, but over a period of months you get to see a transformation as people come to understand the case better.'

Aidan Davy

The DTI commissioned a study measuring the benefit for business competitive advantage from social responsibility and sustainability. The study was organised by *Forum for the Future* in May 2003. The results show that companies engaged in CSR are reporting benefits to their reputation and their bottom line.

The capacity to innovate can be enhanced by both sustainability and social responsibility as can be seen in Vodafone who have developed niche products and overall brand as a result. The conclusion was that CSR made a positive contribution to business success. Those who looked on CSR as a cost rather than an investment in a strategic asset were taking a short term view. They were not taking into consideration how intangibles drive value creation in modern business.

The Government sees CSR as good for society and good for business. In March 2004 Stephen Timms, the Minister responsible for CSR, announced the publication of a draft strategic framework setting out the Government's approach.

Chris Moon and Clive Bonny (2001) say

'There may be short-term costs involved when a business raises its ethical game but, in the longer term, businesses that are trusted and respected by their employees, suppliers, customers and the wider community are more likely than businesses that

are not to provide shareholders with a better return and to be sustainable.'

Taking Action

The Government has launched a new dedicated academy to help CSR take a big leap forward. It is a new resource for organisations of any size wanting to develop their CSR skills and provide a central source of advice and training with the aim of integrating CSR into everyday business practice. It provides the first ever dedicated CSR competency framework and consists of six core characteristics:

- understanding society
- building capacity
- questioning 'business as usual'
- stakeholder relations
- strategic view
- harnessing diversity

Studies from other countries have shown that consistency between policies and actions, the rewarding of ethical behaviour, and executive leadership's attention to ethics has the greatest impact on controlling employees' unethical behaviour.

The Internet

While the Internet allows organisations to forge ever-closer relationships with customers and suppliers, it also poses risks in negligent virus transmission, computer hacking, copyright infringement and email abuse. As well as maximising the use of technology for your business, you need to know how to respond to the misuse of communication technology and how to deal with offenders. You need to have a sound knowledge of the law in managing the ethical risks created by communication technology, and to take conscious responsibility for the flow of information and data in and out of your organisation.

How to set up a CSR programme

The Chartered Institute of Personnel and Development have used material from the Institute of Business Ethics to guide organisations in setting up a CSR Programme.

1. **Find out the company values**

   These are the basic building blocks that underpin business goals. You need to know what the company is about and where it wants to be in the future. It is important to involve employees so there is buy-in to the values

2. **Consider outside help**

   The CSR Academy is a good place to start from

3. **Identify key stakeholders**

   People with a financial or legal agreement, investors, employees, suppliers, customers, the community, the media are all examples.

4. **Assess the situation**

   Do you have a code of practice and does your code of practice or statement of business principles need reviewing. What are other businesses in your sector doing? Does your trade association have a programme that answers your need?

5. **Consider internal disclosure**

   Think about setting up a disclosure mechanism if you don't already have one so staff can raise issues of perceived irresponsible behaviour within the company.

6. **Plan ahead**

   Draft a programme and an implementation plan.

7. **Consult**

   Get comments from the board and all business areas, functions and levels. You may want to use specialist firms if you need to consult on a large scale.

8. **Implementation**

   Publish the programme internally and externally and translate it where appropriate. Communicate and train.

CSR is a strategic issue and is here to stay. In order to stay competitive organisations need to respond and take appropriate action. The shape and focus will depend on the scale and kind of business involved. At the very least CSR brings to our awareness that business operates in a wider community and the interests of that community has to be considered. There is evidence that business is facing up to ethical issues and more support is now available to help implement good practice in our community.

References

Business Ethics – a Guide for Managers, E P Tierney, 1996, Kogan Page, London

Business Ethics – Facing up to the Issues, C Moon & C Bonny 2001, The Economist Books, London

Corporate Social Responsibility and HR's role, Chartered Institute of Personnel and Development , 2003, London

The 21 Irrefutable Laws of Leadership, John C Maxwell, 1998, Thomas Nelson, Nashville

Catherine Carthy
Leadership & Management Development

Catherine has been in the people development industry for 16 years in large multi-nationals—engineering, food processing and packaging. She has also worked in the charity sector and SMEs. She provides powerful leadership, management and personal development programmes designed for busy people who want to get results that last. She has clients in telecoms, banking, finance, publishing, design, public sector, childcare etc. She uses a multi-sensory approach and a combination of delivery methods, i.e., individual coaching, group workshops and self-directed learning to bring her clients results that last.

Catherine has a special interest in business ethics and issues of equality in the workplace.

Bonus Chapter 2

Risk Management
by Doug Hills MBE QGM

Better to have planned for a crisis that doesn't happen than be unprepared for one that does.

Introduction

Businesses today are exposed to a complex range of risks that are numerous and growing. Some are obvious to managers, some are known but their potential impact is underestimated, others lie undetected through lack of awareness or because they are buried deep in the organisation's administration.

Risk Management is a vital element in every business at every level in today's highly competitive, volatile and technological marketplace. This chapter can only scratch the surface and give but a brief introduction to the subject. It is hoped that the reader will not be daunted by the challenges but accept that embracing them is a necessary part of doing business.

Sound Risk Management can deliver the following benefits:

- Legislative and contractual compliance
- Lower insurance costs
- Greater efficiency
- Reduced potential for costly and disruptive events
- Reduced exposure of the business and its directors to litigation

Information risk is a significant one and so a higher degree of emphasis has been given to it.

The risk business

Risk is defined as any source of randomness that may have an impact on the achievement of objectives. It includes risk as an opportunity as well as a threat. Risk is the 'stuff' of business; those organisations that shy away from it (or recklessly believe that it will never happen to them) tend to let fate dictate the future yet we live in uncertain times and the future is even more uncertain.

There are two aspects to every business risk:

- How likely is it to happen?
- What effect will it have on the business?

Risk management is all about managing threats and opportunities. By managing threats effectively the organisation will be in a stronger position to deliver business objectives. By managing opportunities well the organisation will be in a better position to provide improved services and better value for money.

The Risk Management Cycle

When the management of risk goes well it often remains unnoticed. When it fails, however, the consequences can be significant and high-profile; hence the need for effective risk management.

Managing risk is an essential skill in business today. Being the first to market offers great opportunities but also presents many hurdles and therefore risks, including reputational risk. Tesco is a classic example of innovation by being the first with loyalty cards and Internet shopping when both presented risks in terms of:

- Customer take-up versus costs of implementation
- Internet technology being not so robust at the outset coupled with the uncertainty of the increase in home computer use

That Tesco continues to be a leading player in the UK shopping marketplace demonstrates their healthy appetite for, and pro-active management of, risk.

Risk Management has become more sophisticated in recent years as Boards of Directors have come to conclude that they have to take more risks in a highly competitive and difficult marketplace if they are to generate shareholder value. Moreover, all employees have a part to play in achieving this with goals and challenges on risk issues set by directors; but clear ownership and accountability for risk needs to exist at all levels.

High level corporate governance failures, fraud and scandals involving heads of international 'household' names coupled with the catastrophic event of September 11 have raised more than just the profile of risk management; they have also significantly raised insurance premiums around the globe.

Having taken the first step in being pro-active in the management of risk the next is to manage these by:

Avoidance. Can alternative strategies be adopted that will avoid the current risk or eliminate it altogether? For example, the impact of using a particular chemical may cause health and environmental issues and the most appropriate action may be to abstain from using it. However, the introduction of new technology may also remove this and certain other existing risks but it could lead to a new set of risks that would need to be addressed.

Transfer. Insurance is one way to transfer risk but it should be borne in mind that payouts will normally be to set limits on loss of property, stock and earnings over an agreed time frame. Insurance will not cover all intangibles such as lost confidence in the business, lost customers, low staff morale, etc. Can some or all of the risk be transferred to another party?

Retention. Effective action against some risks may be limited, or the cost of taking action may be disproportionate to the potential benefit gained. In this case, the most appropriate course is to monitor the risk to ensure that its likelihood or impact does not change.

Reduction. Can the risk be reduced by a change in procedures or working practices? If new management options arise, it may become appropriate to mitigate the risk through a planned series of measures to reduce and contain the risk to an acceptable level

Pro-active management of risk is beneficial in two ways:

- It allows the Board to make better informed decisions in a riskier marketplace
- It allows insurers to offer significant discounts on premiums because a claim is far less likely.

Information risk

The degree of computerisation in the workplace has led to IT failure becoming one of the most potent operational risks but many businesses blatantly disregard the consequences of inadequate information security measures.

Statistics show that the risks to information security are very real indeed; 90% of businesses that lose data from a disaster are forced to shut within 2 years. If a business is to be serious about managing information risk, the most important step it can take is to understand the risks which include:

- Fraud
- Illegal personal investigation
- Industrial espionage
- Computer viruses

As stated earlier, risk is normally a product of threats and vulnerabilities:

- Threats include:
  - Deliberate manipulation of information prior to input
  - Impersonation of a legitimate user
  - Untrained staff
  - Loss of service
- Vulnerabilities include:
  - Poor website design
  - Slack recruiting procedures
  - Mismanaged computer systems
  - Inadequate staff training

When a business is open to fraud (it may, for example, handle large sums of money), unmanaged vulnerabilities will provide the opportunity for a risk to manifest itself.

The aim of risk management is to reduce such risks to an acceptable level.

Information Risk Statistics

The DTI Information Security Breaches Survey 2002/3 reveals a number of trends that require concerted attention by businesses—especially SMES:

- 44% of UK businesses have suffered at least one malicious security breach in the previous twelve months
- A fifth of these companies took more than a week to recover fully from each incident
- The average cost of each incident was £30,000, with some costing over £500,000
- A third of these incidents were due to virus infections, despite the vast majority of companies using anti-virus software
- Less than 30% of all companies have made a formal commitment to address information security issues
- About half of all businesses do not address Data Protection issues in accordance with the law, a situation that could lead to jail sentences

Information security is a real issue which could have a major impact on every business. To do nothing or pay lip service in this area is folly.

Risk analysis
Risk Analysis allows an organisation to assess threat and compliance issues and the degrees of vulnerability; these are the key factors in determining business continuity management requirements. It should include:
- Identification of risks. For example, damage or denial of access to premises, breaches of statutory requirements, corporate governance
- Appraisal of:
  - The impact of a loss of utilities e.g. electricity, water or gas
  - The failure of business partners or service providers
  - The ramifications of single points of failure within the IT infrastructure. For example, reliance on a single gateway for external communication or the unavailability of key staff

Fortunately, for SMES and branches of national and international businesses in the UK, there are software products that can provide solutions to identifying most of the risks facing most companies. One Business Risks Analysis licensed software system examines the following 15 areas for risk, compliance breaches and vulnerabilities:

- Financials, Customers and Markets
- Employment
- Cash
- Building Maintenance
- Environmental Management
- IT Security
- Vehicle Management
- Contracts & Administration
- Security
- Premises Management
- Health & Safety
- Embezzlement
- Disaster Planning
- Credit Management
- Financial Protection

These are the areas where risk management may be critical to overall business security and viability.

A sample page from the Business Risks Analysis Session
The question appears in blue at the top of the page with multiple choice answers and the option to add a comment which will also appear in the report.

A sample page from the Business Risks Analysis Report

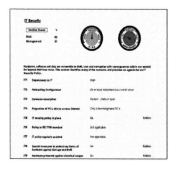

This provides a precise record of the data recorded during the Risk Analysis session.

Two coloured 'barometers' of the degree of risk and the degree of management of each risk for each segment help set priorities and an agenda for action with clear pointers to the steps required.

The company also provides software solutions for client specific Disaster Recovery and Business Continuity Plans.

Conclusions

Risk management is a continuous process and a formal review should take place regularly in order to check the risk profile of the business and there are software, consulting and other solutions available to help all organisations.

Risk management remains a developing discipline that embodies the basic prudence that we can never know the future—we can only prepare for it more intelligently.

Doug Hills

Doug Hills served in the Intelligence Corps and Special Forces for 23 years followed by 11 years in aviation security as the Corporate Security Director of a leading international company. He started his own business in 2000 and has provided security and risk management services to companies of all sizes and in many different sectors such as IT, retail, construction and healthcare.

e-cass provides a range of services including risk analysis, disaster recovery, business continuity planning, security consultancy and investigations.

Interview with
Sir John Harvey Jones

What does success mean to you?

Well, I don't think I've had much success. Because obviously success depends upon the objective you set yourself. If you set yourself, and you always should, a very ambitious objective, in a way, if you achieve it that is failure.

It's the journey that is important not just getting there. You need someone to continuously keep you going, continuously stimulating you to try to do better and different things. Now, really success is a very, very high rate of change, managing to cope with that high rate of change and actually managing to persuade your people to enjoy a high rate of change which is bloody well near impossible.

You served in the Navy. Did the disciplines you learned stand you in good stead for business life?

Oh it was absolutely critical. First of all, you've got to remember I started in the Royal Navy when I was age twelve. So I really was impregnated with Naval values right from the start. Of course the organisation I joined was at that time enormous, and people now don't realise that the Navy in those days was larger than the next two largest navies put together. So it was an enormous outfit, it had very strong ethos very strong values, very strong expectations.

I think probably the thing that I've lived with most, with the Navy, was that they were very slow to praise. They always believed you could do better. The highest praise you could get was, 'Well that was all right but ...' and there was always the 'but', so you were taught never to believe that you've done well, always to believe more should be done. The other thing that you were taught from the age of twelve was that you had to lead by example. The most important people were your troops and the people most expendable were the officers. But I had a bit of good luck during my service in the Navy. First of all I was sunk a couple of times and after that I volunteered for submarines because I figured if I was going to spend a lot of time in the water, it had better be underneath rather than ending up there. Submarines were wonderful, because our crew of 40 people were from every sort of background. This taught me the most important lesson of all, which is that there is practically no limit to what people can achieve if they are given the chance and help. You know, I grew up before the war, when we had a very satisfied society; it was sort of believed that there was an upper class and a working class and so on. Submarines taught me that anybody could do anything if they were given the right background training and expectations.

You joined the Navy aged twelve, but at what point did you realise you could become extremely successful?

Never. I never realised I could achieve things, but I've always realised I want to. If you think that you're doing well, you're in dead trouble. It's rather like living; the day you stop trying to do new and worthwhile things is the day you fall off your bloody bike!

What about young people today, is it the desire to succeed which will get them through?

Well I am both cheered and depressed by kids today. I'm cheered because I think they are of tremendous quality, very good brains, much more liberated, much more free thinking than we were and they need all that. I'm depressed because the single common ground between every one of us in my day, whatever background, was that we all wanted to do something worthwhile. None of us were interested in money; I'm still not, believe it or not. We were all interested in making an impact and helping to make the world a better place, and that's something which for some reason, I don't find amongst the majority of kids. Now there are still some, but the majority of kids set themselves rather prosaic, and I think unambitious and even unworthwhile ambitions. Have you ever met a person who had a lot of money who was (a) an admirable person, and (b) you really envied for their personality and individualism?

You mention the speed of change. Can you expand on why you think companies do not change quickly enough?

It is more difficult to get British companies to move fast than in almost any other country in the world. We have a national picture of Nirvana, as tomorrow being the same as yesterday, but maybe with better pay and a bit more comfort. In reality all change is uncomfortable and you therefore have to relish discomfort in order to move on faster to the better world. You will never change unless you believe you are going to change into a better world. But the big difference now is modern communications, modern technology, the digital age, the Internet etc. are really genuinely making the world one place. It's difficult to remember that when I was in England as a boy, life used to be limited to your village or your county town. Now you can't make a living as a business, trying to serve a village or a county town, you can barely make a living as a business trying to serve Britain. You need to at least be serving Europe, but even serving Europe is not enough.

How good is the standard of leadership in the UK today?

I think we're suffering a crisis in leadership in the UK and have been for some years. You've only got to think who our heroes are now, pop stars, not individuals who achieve unbelievable things with very little going for them. Leadership has to be judged against achievement and, in particular, against the achievement of enabling ordinary people to achieve extraordinary things, by growing people. Part of the problem is that people think that leadership is only inherited, which it's not, or just taught, which it's also not. It's a combination of the two.

What I eventually realised was a lot of leaders I had admired were actually just the same as all the rest of us, with just as many weaknesses, they just had bigger bloody jobs.

There are three characteristics that I recognise in outstanding leaders that I have known, and I have known an enormous array. The first one is that they are tough as old boots. One of my great heroes was Nelson. Not a nice man, and he was always having bits fall off him, but tough as old boots and that is a combination of being able to work very, very long hours, concentrate for a long time and be intellectually rigorous and tough. That's the first one. The second one is an ability to communicate and that means both to hear and to speak. There are an awful lot of examples of leaders who lack ears and their communication skills are very much outwards, rather than inwards. I believe that the key to successful leadership is to have both. Lastly, every leader has to have a dream or vision of where they are going. You have to have a vision and a dream of where you're trying to get to, and know how you're going to help other people to share in that dream.

If you were twelve again, what would your dream and vision be?

Well, I would hope I would have had the same vision as I did then. Actually, I have dreamed now for many, many years of having a country where economic and business performance match our native genius but for some reason, we have never managed to realise this. I believe we are an outstanding group of people, but for some reason, I don't know, we never seem to get it together, to really achieve what we are capable of. I've been trying for many years to put my pennyworth in to improve both the ability of our businesses, small business people in particular, and the recognition of how important they are to all of us.

||||||||||||||||||||||||||||||||||||||||||||||||||||||||||||||||||||||||

Sir John Harvey-Jones, MBE, was born in England, spending his early childhood in India, and returned to school in England at the age of six. He was educated at the Royal Naval College at Dartmouth, and served in the Royal Navy form 1937 to 1956. He worked for ICI from 1956 to 1987, for the last five years as its Chairman.

Sir John has since served on the boards of many companies, public bodies and charities, including *The Economist* newspaper, Grand Metropolitan plc and the Royal Society of Arts. From 1986 to 1991 he was Chancellor of Bradford University.

||||||||||||||||||||||||||||||||||||||||||||||||||||||||||||||||||||||||

Watch this video interview plus many more like it through your free subscription to online business TV portal Expertsonline.tv available to you as a buyer of this book. Just send an e-mail to **info@expertsonline.tv**, *including the ISBN number, and the location of where you bought the book to receive your free subscription worth £50.*

www.expertsonline.tv

Bonus Chapter 3

Healthy and Safe, an Essential Element for Success
by Alan Coulson

An essential element of making your business work for you is to have effective control of Health and Safety in order to:

- Control the cost of accidents which can be equal to 5% of operating costs; and
- Minimize the risk of enforcement action disrupting or stopping work activities.

The conclusion of an HSE study on the financial cost of accident was that:" … *few companies had any idea just what accidents at work really cost them, nor the means to find out.*"

Cost of Accidents
Introduction
The financial losses arising from accident in most organisations is excessive, leaking away valuable resources and cutting profitability. It is essential that all organisations effectively tackle this issue for the sake of the well being of their balance sheets and their employees. The result of an HSE study showed that losses can be equivalent to 37% of profits or 5% of operating costs.

It is important to realise that the term "accident" in the context of this chapter (and the HSE study referred to below) includes work related deaths, injuries, ill health and damage. Statistics that are widely available show that the financial losses arising from damage accidents is significant in most organisations.

Study on cost of accidents

The Health and Safety Executive first published HSG96 (*The cost of accidents at work* —HSG96, HSE Books) in 1993 to report on their findings following the study on cost of accidents. An updated report was published in 1997 and this is available from HSE Books and good retail booksellers.

The overall conclusion of the study was that: " *...few companies had any idea just what accidents at work really cost them, nor the means to find out.*"

The study looked at the cost of accidents in the five work situations including a Construction site, a Creamery and a Transport Company. The study found that the ratio of insured cost to uninsured cost ranged from 1:8 to 1:36 (i.e. for every £1 covered by insurance there were between £8 and £36 which was uninsured). At the time of the study there were no very serious accidents that could have distorted the findings.

For those wishing to obtain an accurate picture of the level of accident losses, HSG96 contains a form that can be used to determine actual costs incurred.

The following are some examples from the author's experience that support the HSE findings.

Practical example 1

When undertaking an assessment of the management system used in the service industry, It was recommended that they either determined the actual cost of accidents that occur or estimate it on a frequent basis and report this information to senior management.

As a result of this advice, their conservative estimate of their accident losses was as follows:-

Estimate of cost of accidents	£2,400,000/yr
Approximate number of employee	2,000
Average (conservative) cost of accidents per employee	£1,200/yr

Practical example 2

A small construction company employing about 65 employees had an accident which resulted in one employee sustaining serious head injuries that have left him with a permanent disability. It is estimated that the uninsured losses associated with this accident alone resulted in a reduction in profit of about some 25% in the year when the accident occurred.

Unlike large organisations, with small companies there may be few visible signs of accident losses until a bad accident occurs. The situation with large organisations is usually clearer because dangerous incidents and accidents will be happening more frequently due to the larger number of employees exposed to any work related risks.

People related benefits

The financial losses referred to above are unacceptable, as is the pain and suffering caused by work related deaths, injuries and ill-health. Any reduction in the pain and suffering that accidents cause will be welcomed by employers, Trade Unions, employees and their families and is likely to improve moral and Industrial Relations to the benefit of the business.

Why is industry generally not addressing this issue

This information has been available now for over 10 years, yet many businesses are still unaware of financial costs arising from accidents. Even a relatively small reduction in accident losses sustained by a business—say 10%—would have a significant impact on operating costs and profits. But what about suppliers and contractors that provide equipment, materials and services ? They are likely to be sustaining similar losses, if a Company could get their suppliers and Contractors to take a similar approach to reduce accident losses then the cost of equipment, materials and services to the business could also be reduced.

In any other area of business operations, losses of the magnitude highlighted by the HSE study would result in

Directors initiating an urgent study to determine why the losses were occurring and what changes could be made to ensure that effective control of the losses was established and maintained.

Effective management of OH&S
Since 1992 the Management of Health and Safety at Work Regulations has required that all employers use accepted management principles to manage Health and Safety.

The following are the four key matters that need to be in place to ensure the effective management of Health and Safety:-
1.   A genuine management commitment to H&S needs to exist;
2.   Arrangements to measure H&S performance;
3.   An effective H&S management system to ensure accepted management principles are being applied.
4.   An understanding of accepted H&S management principles.

These issues will be examined below in more detail.

Getting the H&S culture right
If Directors and Managers of an organisation have a genuine commitment to Health and Safety then this will be apparent in their actions day by day and will therefore greatly assist in the development and maintenance of a positive Health and Safety culture within the business. Employees at all levels are very skilled at determining what their superiors really want irrespective of the words they say. Paying lip service to Health and Safety is easily recognised by employees and so is a genuine commitment.

The first step in getting the required culture in place is to define what it should be and then communicate this to personnel by inclusion of a suitable statement in the Health and Safety Policy and in any employees briefing system. An example of a suitable statement would be as follows:

"The Directors and managers are fully committed to Health and Safety and will ensure that:

- ◆ "It is integrated into normal business practice;
- ◆ "It is established as being of equal importance to other business functions;
- ◆ "A top down management approach is used to manage Health and Safety; and
- ◆ "Directors and managers will lead by example."

Such statement must only be made if there is a genuine desire to take steps to ensure the full and effective adherence to the above principles. So how is it possible to determine if individual Directors and Managers are complying with the above? The answer is to manage the situation in the same way as any other business activity by:

- • Determining the best way of recognising when a Director or Manager is applying these principles;
- • Establish arrangements to check on a regular basis that Directors and Managers are acting in the expected way; and
- • Provide feedback on any misalignment between behaviours observed and those expected.

When Directors and Managers are seen to act in a manner that is consistent with the declared culture, it will be relatively easy to get others to act in a similar manner. This process will lead to the development of a strong positive Health and Safety culture.

Measuring H&S Performance

Traditionally Health and Safety has been managed mainly on the basis of past failures that have occurred i.e based on the use of accident statistics. This would be like managing quality on the basis of the customer complaints and is clearly not an effective management approach.

"What gets measured gets done" is so true, but the most important measurement data to use is that from active measures of performance rather than reactive measures such as accident data. With the management of other business functions active measurement data is always available and used, but with Health and Safety in most situations there is a serious lack of any systems for determining active measures of performance.

But how do we measure performance? In relation to the management and control of Health and Safety culture considered above, it is possible to identify a number of factors that will enable the actions / behaviours of Directors and Managers to be monitored and assessed. In order to measure performance all we need to do is apply a scoring system to the actions / behaviours being monitored and use these to determine a measure of performance in relation to the level of adherence to the required culture.

A similar process can be adopted for measuring performance against accepted management principles (BS 8800 or OHSAS 18001) and specific Health and Safety Regulations such as COSHH, Manual Handling, Display Screen Equipment etc.

Once a system has been established for measuring performance with respect to a number of Health and Safety issues, the availability of active performance data makes the management process much easier and much more effective.

Do managers know how to manage effectively

When managers are promoted into a new role or move jobs, in the main they will find themselves slotted into an existing management structure with existing arrangements in place to manage their operational role. They would rarely find themselves in a situation without any systems for monitoring and reporting on production output, materials utilization, production line / process efficiency, cost control, overheads, customer complaints etc. Most managers therefore have little need to maintain a good working knowledge of the accepted management principles and there application and benefits to the management process.

In contrast to this, although the law requires that accepted management principles are applied to the management of

Health and Safety this is still rarely applied and there is little experience of the arrangements and systems necessary to apply these principles. It is therefore not surprising that managers are often at a loss to know how to proceed with the management of Health and Safety.

All key managers need to have a good understanding of the management principles contained in BS8800 and OHSAS 18001 and need to able to demonstrate to the Enforcing Authorities or the Courts that they are being applied. Due to the general lack of understanding of accepted management principles, the only practical way to achieve this is to have a structured Health and Safety Management System that will help Directors and Managers apply the principles.

H&S Management System

Ask about an organization's Health and Safety Management System and in most cases you will be presented with large files containing a mass of related Policies, procedures and arrangements that should be implemented and maintained. In practice Managers rarely have the time or inclination to read, understand and implement the contents of large amounts of documented information and it is therefore doomed to failure.

The mass of paperwork referred to above actually obstructed the implementation of the necessary procedures and arrangements contained in them. In contrast a software based system developed and used by the author proved to be very successful and enabled managers at all levels to manage Health and Safety effectively with the application of the minimum of resources. The features of the system are as follows:

- covers the implementation of the management principles contained in BS 8800 / OHSAS 18001;
- covers relevant Health and Safety Policies, Standards and best practice;
- provides an effective vehicle to communicate legal and organizational requirements to relevant personnel;

- incorporates a method of measuring performance against requirements;
- enables line managers to review / assess performance on a regular basis;
- can be used for independent auditing of performance;
- gives guidance on corrective action necessary to achieve compliance / improve performance;
- the system can be updated and improved in line with continuous improvement requirements.

Directors and Managers at all levels found the software system to be very user friendly and the end result was that Health and Safety performance was driven forward rapidly with the use of minimum time and other resources.

Where to start

In what order should the four items referred to initially be implemented? The most effective approach is to implement in the order they are listed for the following reasons:-

1. The right commitment / culture must come first because without this any effort applied to the development of Health and Safety will be undermined by the lack of support / interest.
2. Decide on how to measure Health and Safety performance. Active measures of performance are such a powerful tool—it is true that what gets measured gets done. In my experience a few % measures of performance has 10 times the impact that any written report would have.
3. Decide on a structured management system that facilitates the application of accepted management principles. (Usually this would be linked with the means of measuring performance.)
4. Take care with items 2 and 3 above. The right system will have a significant impact and it is important to plan and manage these changes carefully to achieve the maximum benefits.

Alan Coulson

Alan Coulson has 20 plus years experience providing H&S advice and support to organisations ranging from blue chip multi-nationals to SMES.

Alan is accomplished in devising and implementing practical, effective systems to satisfy H&S requirements with minimum interference with core business activities and maximum benefits in terms of risk reduction and cost. Recognised as providing a competent, practical, value added service.

www.expertsonline.tv

Bonus Chapter 4

Are you getting your message across?
by Andy Fogg

A friend of mine was once involved in a fiendishly complicated bit of internal politics. He was having an email dialogue with senior managers about a significant sales contract. Knowing that he needed his immediate boss's support, he made sure that he copied his manager on every email.

After a week of email exchanges it was clear that he was not getting the back up he needed from his manager. It was time to find out why. He walked into his boss's office and challenged him about the lack of support. "But I haven't seen any emails," claimed his boss. "Well I copied you on every one," said my friend. "Ah," said his boss, "that's why then. I don't read cc mails, only ones addressed directly to me."

Are your colleagues listening? How did your boss react to your latest report? Do you expect senior management to approve your latest initiative? Will your client see the value of your proposal? Not getting your message across can be a costly business.

Try the email test
Here's another thought or two about email. How many emails did you get today? No, this isn't a macho competition, but I bet it's a big number. OK, now think about those emails. How many did you delete without reading past the subject or the first line? Come on, it was a big number too, wasn't it? Then there are the cc mails that didn't seem that

relevant. Now take away all those that you read, but didn't feel compelled to do anything about.

So, how many are left? No, this isn't one of those 'think of a number' conundrums where I can tell you the answer—just how many *are* left? How many emails actually persuaded you to do something? Well, I'd lay odds on it being a small number and definitely a small number as a proportion of the big number you started with—right?

Learn from the mistakes of others

Why did these people waste their time sending these to you? In business, there's only one reason to write—to get someone to take action. Clearly these people failed. They didn't get their message across and they weren't persuasive.

Could the same be happening to you or your team?

It's as much as a 90% failure rate

I've asked a lot of people these questions and reached the conclusion that up to 90% of all written communications fail. They just don't get the result the author was looking for. That's only one in every ten emails, letters or reports that actually gets its message across and drives some action. Want to know why?

… and the reason is …

OK, let me explain, but you'll need to put your brain into consultant mode. All consultants use two-by-two matrices. Consultants can reduce everything to a two-by-two matrix. You know the idea. It's where you get four quadrants and the place to be, the sweet spot, is always the top right! So, here goes.

Only 10% of written communications drive action

FOCUS	Stream of consciousness	Well crafted
Reader-centred	Missed opportunity 10%	Drive action 10%
Writer-centred	Binned or deleted 65%	Nice to know 15%

Stream of consciousness   Well crafted   **CLARITY**

Is it crystal clear?

Let's label the horizontal axis 'clarity'. We need to ask ourselves, what is it about a document that makes the message crystal clear?

Well, it's when the writer has thought about the structure of the thing. The arguments have some logical flow. They are spelled out in simple English, with short sentences and paragraphs. Topic changes are signposted with meaningful headlines and the layout looks as good as the words sound. A good description of such a document is 'well crafted' and this is the label we'll use for the right hand end of the clarity axis.

Or as clear as mud?

At the other end of the scale is that typical email—the brain dump. There's little chance of following the logic, let alone spotting any fragments of ideas in the torrent of prose. You know the sort of thing. I'll call it 'stream of consciousness' and this labels the far left end of our horizontal axis.

Does it persuade ...

'Focus' is the label of the vertical axis. A document involves two people—the writer and the reader. Will the reader's view of life always match the writer's? Absolutely not—as my friend found out with his boss's views on cc mails.

So I'm going to label the top end of the vertical axis 'reader-centred'. Here the writer has thought through everything he possibly can about the reader. He's considered the reader's

- role
- knowledge of the topic
- reaction to the subject matter
- use of the document
- ability to act.

Most importantly the writer has thought about why he is writing. The writer is very clear on what action he wants the reader to take and has thought about why the reader would go out of their way to act—about what's in it for them?

... or bore to death?

At the bottom end of the vertical scale is the opposite—'writer-centred'. Here the writer doesn't think about the reader at all. He only thinks about his own situation and perspective—about what he wants to say, not what the reader may need to hear.

Hitting the sweet spot

Putting these four labels on our two-by-two gives us our four quadrants. So let's consider what happens with a document that sits in any of these.

The sweet spot is pretty obvious isn't it? A well-crafted and reader-centred document stands the best chance of getting a result. The reader can understand the well-presented arguments and can warm to them as they are in his terms and persuade him to take action.

Well thanks ... now moving on ...
What about the bottom right quadrant? Here we have a well-crafted document, but it is writer-centred. So, the arguments are clear but they're from the writer's perspective which means they may not hit home with the reader. I like to think of this quadrant as being the 'nice to know' box. Thanks for telling me all that, but I'm not going to do anything. Our cc mails fit in here.

What on earth is all this about?
Top left? This is reader-centred but in stream of consciousness mode. What chance has the reader of spotting what's in it for him? This is the 'missed opportunity' box. You had it all worked out but blew it in a haze of confusion.

Ding—document deleted
So to the bottom left. This is the worst of all worlds—not only writer-centred but in stream of consciousness style. You know what you do with emails like this don't you? Your finger goes straight to the delete button. Any document in this box ends up in the bin. Worse still, so might the next one from the same writer—because a reputation precedes it.

Which pigeonhole do you fit in?
I said earlier that I'd asked lots of people about documents that drive action. Their answers are a warning to us all. When asked to pigeonhole the writing they see from their teams and their peers, they tell me that

- only about 10% hit the sweet spot and drive action
- some 15% to 25% appear in the bottom right—nice to know
- another 10% to 20% are in the top left—missed opportunities
- between 50% and 60% are in the bottom left—the worst place to be.

A costly business

So back to the last report you put in to your boss or your latest sales proposal. Did you get the result you wanted? Not getting your message across can be a costly business. It's actually a triple whammy. You waste the time you spent writing the document, you waste the time your reader spent reading it but, most importantly, you fail to get your result.

You can fix all three problems

You don't have to be Shakespeare to write well-crafted, reader-centric documents—anyone can do it. You'll save your readers valuable time, you'll use yours profitably and best of all you'll get your message across.

Are you producing second-rate proposals?

Many consultancy proposals end up being second-rate— yes, it's a generalisation, but a pretty accurate one in my experience.

What do I mean by second-rate? Well, in simple terms, a proposal that

- takes too much time to read and understand
- lacks a clear and compelling message
- appears to be more about the writer (supplier) than the reader (client).

Where the problems usually start— with multiple authors

In large consultancy projects, the most common reason for second-rate proposals is 'multiple authors'. The difficulties are well known. Having more than one author

- produces mixed styles and messages that confuse the reader
- introduces ownership issues that cause friction and delay
- brings editing and review cycles that are hard to manage

... and end—with a rushed management summary
All of these problems threaten deadlines and end with a rushed management summary. What should be the most powerful and useful part of the proposal suddenly becomes the weakest.

Although all these difficulties are clear, the solutions are not. Most organisations don't have a way of 'writing' proposals—it's more that they just cobble them together.

How you can do things differently?
It is possible to make your life easier—even with multiple authors. The answers revolve around a small number of key business-writing concepts and how you manage them. In other words—having a writing process.

Focus on your reader or readers
We all know that you have to understand your client before you can sell effectively. However, when we write we seem to forget the obvious parallel—that we need to understand our reader. Clarifying our knowledge of the reader is an important first step in any writing process. Communicating that knowledge effectively to all the authors is crucial if the final document is to be consistently reader-focused.

Deliver a compelling message
Quality proposals carry a clear and unambiguous message. Achieving this brings a number of challenges, particularly with multiple authors. These are:
1. agreeing the compelling message at the beginning
2. communicating it clearly to all authors
3. monitoring its delivery throughout the proposal.

A good writing process helps with all of these challenges.

Make it easy to read and understand
We are all readers as well as writers. How good is your attention span when reading a lengthy sales proposal? More importantly, how good is your reader's? Have you noticed

that there seems to be a close link between attention span and seniority!

Many consultants fall in to the trap of producing 'gobbledygook'. They write long flowery sentences, thinking that they sound intelligent and knowledgeable. This 'consultese' simply puts readers to sleep.

Making your proposal easy to read requires sound editing skills. Easy to read content doesn't just help you get your message across. It also improves productivity by reducing the reading and review time in your bid process. A writing process should provide editing rules, tools for document review and a common language for authors and reviewers.

You need a writing process

A writing process is not the same as a proposal or bid process. You may have sophisticated management tools and excellent project management but this doesn't help you to customise the proposal's content. The content must focus on the client's needs, be easy to read and deliver a consistent and compelling message. A writing process helps you do this.

How it fits alongside your existing bid process

Your writing process needs to fit beside your proposal or bid process. But how do you link them—especially with multiple authors? Here's how you might do it.

How the writing process works with multiple authors

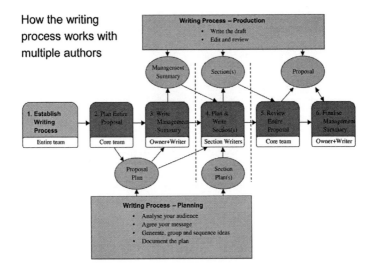

1. **Establish your 'reader-centred' writing process**

   All authors and reviewers need to be familiar with the writing process. This is more than just being familiar with some business-writing skills. The process should bring with it a common language that allows a team to be efficient and accurate when discussing a document. Using this language helps to avoid any sense of personal criticism that would otherwise creep in when reviewing and editing.

2. **Plan the entire proposal**

   The core team should develop the proposal plan. First, they review the client profile and focus on the targeted readers of the proposal. Then, using the tools and strategies provided by the writing process, the team
   - brainstorms and signs off the main messages
   - captures bullet points under agreed headlines for each section
   - sequences the headlines to produce the proposal's structure
   - assigns authors to each section.

3. **Write a draft management summary**

One person can now write a draft management summary using this plan. He or she will use the tools and strategies from the writing process to help draft, edit and review the document.

Writing a draft management summary at this stage tests the plan and helps to refine it. The result also acts as a

a) checkpoint for the core team to sign off—on both content and tone

b) template for section authors to use—in terms of style

c) context for section authors—providing alignment with the proposal's key messages.

4. **Plan and write each section**

Each section author now has two agreed inputs to help them—the top-level plan and the draft management summary.

With these guidelines, they can use the planning stages of the writing process iteratively—at the section level, at the sub-section level and even at the paragraph level.

Finally, section authors use the writing process to draft and edit their sections, before offering them up for review.

5. **Review the entire proposal**

Once all section authors have submitted their drafts, the core team can review the entire proposal. The common language of the writing process helps the team review the document as a group. They can easily provide constructive criticism to section authors where changes are necessary.

6. **Finalise the management summary**

In a large and complex bid, some elements of the solution and approach may change during the bid process. The draft management summary will need to reflect these changes. The original author will revise the draft and produce the final management summary.

Give it a try with your next proposal

The tools and techniques in a good writing process will be based on common sense—as many of the best ideas are. However, it is the way these elements come together—as a recipe for success—that delivers value.

Inserting a writing process into your bid process is just common sense too. Why not give it a try?

Andy Fogg

Andy has over thirty years experience in sales, marketing, consulting and general management roles. He has set up and run a training company and has worked in information technology, call-centre outsourcing and management consultancy organisations. His speciality is winning business with the shortest possible proposals.

Bonus Chapter 5

How to make your wishes come true.
(Project management)

by Penny Lowe

Looking back at the New Year's resolutions you have made, which ones have you achieved? For most people it is those where they have set themselves clear stages to achieve by definite dates, and they have had a clear reason for doing it.

The same is true in business. Your goal may be to implement new accounting software, develop a marketing campaign to sell a new product or simply to ensure that all staff have a performance review before the date of the annual pay review. The first stage is to identify the goal.

At this stage project management has already begun. To identify the desired outcome allows you to judge whether or not you have achieved it.

Clarifying your goal

One management theory is that any objective set should be SMART. The same applies to your goals. For each goal you need to be *specific*. This means there is no room for uncertainty or lack of focus.

If the goal is to expand the product range, you may not know at the start what the new product is. This is actually untrue. You may not know the name of the product but you do know what you expect it to achieve. Are you looking for a complementary product, a replacement product or a product to allow you to diversify into other areas? What percentage of total revenue do you expect it contribute? How much of a contribution do you need to the bottom line?

If you asked an inexperienced member of staff to do the research, what would you need to tell them in order to get a short list that was acceptable to you? Whether it is a member of staff or you who are looking at expanding the product range, these questions need answering before you begin or you will waste significant time and energy. A common trap for some businesses is the senior executives knowing what they want but failing to communicate it. If it is identified at the top level and documented, there is no room for misunderstanding. As with all things, the preparation will take time and effort but not as much time or ill feeling as work being done on the wrong things.

The next element is that a goal should be *measurable*. With the new product example, how much of total business are you expecting it to bring in? Answering this will allow you to test whether it has achieved its target. It may be that the new product is needed to attract business and is designed to be a loss leader. Everyone will be happy if this was stated at the start and the measurement is to increase overall turnover by x or the number of new customers in the next twelve months by y. In the same way, if a stated purpose is to add a fixed value to the bottom line, the best way may be to out source production and support of the product until sales increase to a specific value to support additional fixed costs.

Be realistic. To set up a profitable outlet in China within three months may be possible for some businesses, but very few could achieve a profit within three months. Although this may be an unlikely goal for your business, is what you are aiming for feasible?

One of the most common reasons for failure is not allocating sufficient funds to the project from the start. Before any project is sanctioned to proceed there should be a feasibility study. Is the desired outcome *attainable*? If the feasibility study shows that you need to spend quarter of a million before you see any returns, that is not a problem. Instead the question can be asked as to where this money could come from. If it is a great aunt, fine, she may not ask many questions. If it is a lending institution such as a bank, they will want a full and detailed business plan. If it is a venture capital organisation, they may want a share in the company. How much is it worth to you to achieve the goal? I am not saying that you cannot achieve the extreme, only that you must recognise what is needed and act accordingly.

When reading some management books, you may find that 'R' stands for 'realistic'. I believe this is covered in many areas by 'attainable'. I prefer the use of 'R' as 'relevant'. Life is short enough without wasting effort on irrelevant activities. I choose to distinguish here between wasting time and spending time. To take on a school student for two weeks work experience may cost money because of the time staff spend explaining what they are doing and being patient while the student tries things for themselves. However, you may choose to do it as you wish to raise the profile of the industry, hoping the word will spread as to how wonderful your organisation is to work for, or simply because you have a wish to help the local school. These are all good reasons why you may choose to be diverted from your core business. The difference is that it is a choice. In order to stay within time and budget on a project, each activity should be judged as to whether it is *relevant*.

Is it appropriate to have this goal at this time? If you know that the compliance laws are due to change at the start of next year, are you trying to take advantage of a window of opportunity, or is it your goal to ensure you comply on day one of the new legislation? If the new product launch is for sun hats, and the target market is the United Kingdom holiday maker, should the product launch be planned for November? Again some books will refer to the 'T' as 'timely' others will use 'time constrained'. It does not matter which you use—the purpose is to challenge the goal to ensure it is clearly stated.

So a SMART goal should be specific, measurable, attainable, relevant and timely. An example of a smart objective is to make six sales of a large product (already defined by the company) with a total value of at least €300,000 within the next fifteen months at a cost of less than €185,000—the cost to include cost of goods, marketing, salaries and related overheads.

By defining the goal in this way, it will be easy in sixteen months to look back and judge whether the goal was achieved. With a plan you will know whether you are on track before you reach the end.

'To fail to have a plan is to plan to fail'

Going back to New Year resolutions, many people will get to the following year realising they have not achieved what they wanted. If you then ask the question 'did they plan how they would achieve their goals and objectives?' the answer is usually no.

The same is true of achieving goals in the workplace. You may want to have a meeting to tell staff of a bonus resulting from the success of a project. Even this will need planning if it is to be successful. Finding out when staff are in, giving them sufficient notice, making sure the venue is accessible to all and knowing what is going to be said. The meeting can go ahead without all these factors being considered but it will defeat its purpose of thanks and motivation if you are the only person that turns up.

The starting point for a plan is a brain dump of all the tasks involved. By using this as a skeleton, items within the initial list may prompt other thoughts. So often tasks are omitted because they are not part of the standard flow of activities. These can be the ones to catch people out particularly when needing to use outside resources. One classic is allowing sufficient time for printed material to be proof read as well as being printed. Whether it is a brochure, business cards or training course notes they all need to have the printer's proofs checked and scheduled into their work plans.

Tasks can be taken off the list when justified but shouldn't be added to the list without good cause as the consequences can ruin the feasibility of the project. If the project is time constrained, e.g. the need to deliver to a customer by a specific date, penalties may be imposed for late delivery costing more than the total profit for the job. Or the missing task may be to obtain funding which, with the banks requiring due diligence checks, may mean that even when a lender says yes, it will be another two months before the money is transferred into your account.

A plan should be far more than simply the tasks. Each task needs a start date and duration. More than that, it also needs a cost, resource and quality level. This may be more than you usually associate with tasks, but one can go further and start to document the possible risks associated with each task. The most obvious one is that a task is dependent on the one before. There are many others; each should be documented and the consequences of possible outcomes should be measured.

Professional project managers will refer to the task list as the project schedule. The other documents all go to make up the project plan. These include the business case, project objective, risk register, quality management system and a change control register. In larger projects it is not uncommon to have a project librarian. This is not administration for its own sake, but a function that allows you to monitor and review.

A plan is there to be reviewed and modified

Having created a plan, it should not be treated like a picture calendar, just an excuse to have pictures on the wall. It should be a living document of which everyone is aware, to which everyone contributes and which is updated with progress and any changes on a regular basis. One criticism I heard is that managers at a large construction company never get to see the whole plan. They are given their bit with a deadline and they have no indication of the interaction with other parts of the project. Experience has taught them that the completion dates they are given are not the actual dates on the schedule but perhaps their manager trying to build in some slack. This is all very well but has resulted in unecessary pressure leading to false deadlines being missed and ignored causing a lack of trust on both sides.

To understand where your contribution fits in to the whole allows you to highlight problems and make suggestions. This is not to say that every party needs to know the full details, but those with influence over an area must understand that part and where the major tasks fit into the overall plan.

If staff are away, move on or are re-assigned within the company, the plan may well need to change. The extent of the change will then allow a cost to be associated with that change. To move a member of staff internally and decide to take on contract staff to do the work of the individual may incur expensive contractor's fees, time lost through bringing them up to speed and the loss of knowledge to the organisation when the contractor leaves. On evaluation it may be better for the project to keep the member of staff on the project and hire a contractor to do the other work the employee was being asked to do in the short term.

Unless a plan exists, it cannot be used and reviewed. Some people ask why create a plan when you know it will change? The answer is that the effect of the change can be measured more effectively. A schedule drawn up with week numbers rather than dates can be more use when the project is subject to Board approval as there is no guarantee at which monthly meeting it will be considered. The risk summary submitted with it can state the factors affecting the start and finish dates and any windows of opportunity. Once the initial plan has been approved, it can then be revisited for actual dates to be added and statutory holidays to be included.

As with your personal diary, events occur that cause a change in plan—so is the case with the project schedule.

With a documented plan, the effects of these changes can be understood and action taken accordingly.

Don't work backwards from a deadline

In practice many projects fail, or do not fully achieve their goals, because they do not plan their route. If you are embarking on a journey, you have more chance of arriving on time by deciding what stages make up the journey, how long each will take and then deciding on the total time. This can then be compared with the deadline. It may be the check in time for a flight is the deadline. In this case, you would plan each stage of your journey including parking and getting to the airport terminal from the car park. From this you decide what time you will need to start out.

It may appear that this is working backwards from a deadline, but as the thinking process has been forwards on the journey, the risk of stages being overlooked has been lessened.

When there is a deadline, this can be part of the planning process. By constraining time, budget and resource may need to be extended. By recognising this, a value can then be put on the need to achieve the deadline. A simple example is travelling by train to a meeting. By arranging a meeting half an hour later, you can then travel on a cheap day return ticket on the train. Some of the benefits are cost saving and comfort when travelling on a less crowded train. How much will be lost by this simple adjustment to a deadline? If it is a course or conference being attended it may be difficult to move the start time. If it is an exam, your planning process will take more seriously the risk factors that can affect your journey. This is where materiality starts to become a factor.

Every project should have a deadline but arrived at by working forward. The benefit of a schedule is that it has short term goals (milestones), dates and deliverables along the way. By also treating these as deadlines, the project is more likely to stay on track and reach its end goal. If problems are arising they can be corrected rather than compounded.

Check regularly

Meetings for the sake of meetings just waste time, but if they are to monitor progress then they can be justified. Many of the facts can be found out and circulated before the meeting but a regular meeting to present the position to date can be a good way of focusing the mind. It is just as important to share good news as it is bad.

One benefit of regular checks is to ensure that the purpose is still justified and that the goal is still realistic.

Focus on the goal

In the software industry, projects have traditionally been delivered late, or are of poor quality. One reason for this is known as scope creep. I know many builders of private residences have met the same problem. "Wouldn't it be nice if ..." causes a developer of software or builder of houses to cringe. The moment they hear this they know that the customer's expectations are changing and so, there fore, is the cost of delivery. There may be exceptions to this but they are very few and far between.

It is easy to be diverted into areas of personal interest or quick fixes. Each of these needs to be treated as a project in its own right—a business case made, feasibility considered and resources found. The biggest danger from this cause of project failure is for a small business, where controls are not in place and change management is an unheard of concept.

A larger project should have a change management system built in. Companies who do well are those who are commercially minded but friendly with it. If you ask your builder to change all the doors in the main house to match those being put in the extension while it is being built, he needs to agree with you the types of door and door furniture required; who will be painting/treating them; the extra cost and the effect on the expected completion date. Giving you a quote on this basis, i.e. a separate job, will allow you to recognise the effect of the change request and decide whether you really want him to go ahead with all or part of the request. You should also find out by when you need to make your decision.

This approach allows focus to be kept on the original project until a decision is made. The necessary changes can then be made to the order for parts, for labour and for the delivery date. Most importantly there will be no shocks for customer or supplier when the final price is calculated.

To test whether the project is still focused on the goal. Study the objectives, are they still going to be achieved.

The business case

Don't start what you can't finish.

The goal should have been clearly defined at the start together with a business case. Many people view the business case as the justification for setting up the project. Although this is true, it should also be used as the test as to whether the project should continue.

When a known point in a project (a milestone) is reached, this can often be a good point to reassess the purpose and viability of the project. If staff have left and contractors are having to be employed to keep on target, is there still the possibility of a profit at the end? Would it be cheaper to employ staff on a short term contract till the end of the project rather than weekly contractors and spending time and effort trying to employ permanent staff who cannot see a long term future?

Have the customer requirements changed to wanting customised work rather than a common product that you could sell on to others to cover development costs?

There are many factors that can affect the business case and it is always too late to leave it to post project review to see where things went wrong.

With a small business, the biggest cause for change to a business case is initial optimism rather than realism. Whether you feel that you can continue to get your raw materials from other people's scrap or whether your daughter will work free of charge to help the family business, if these do not happen, it can add considerably to your costs. Home cooked cakes make a good price but when you need to spend thousands to have your domestic kitchen passed as a commercial area for food preparation, is it really justified? Are you going to make the profit that caused you to go into business in the first place?

As well as the increase in costs, a reduction in the market sector or price cutting can reduce your potential sales income. If you sell luxury goods in an area where thousands of people are about to be made redundant, you may find your target market is watching its pennies and cuts out expenditure on exactly the products you sell.

The importance of reviewing why the project is being undertaken cannot be underestimated. To continue with plans to move offices when the firm is about to be bought out can result in costs for no gain. Don't just bury your head in the sand, recognise what is going on around you.

A final measure of the justification for a project is the analysis of not doing the project. This should also be taken seriously as it can influence your justification for undertaking it. A simple example is not moving offices when the lease runs out. Are you intending to be a squatter? What penalties would you incur? What will be the effect on the business? Again, having a business case to consider is important even if only to confirm that alternative action is beneficial.

Recognise the risks

For any project there should be a risk register. Although this seems very formal, it is better to recognise areas in advance and prepare contingencies than to compromise the project. Each risk can be given a probability and a consequence with a resulting score. The highest risks being reviewed regularly and the lesser risks being reviewed to ensure their score has not changed.

People can often be critical of risk assessment and claim it gets in the way. What they forget are the consequences of not assessing risks.

Do not send all your chief engineers in the same minibus to Blackpool the weekend before a big client meeting. If you are reliant on the charisma of the founder to keep customers and staff on board, consider key man insurance. If a lecture tour has only one possible speaker, decide what you would do if they were unwell or stranded in a different country due to the weather.

These things may never happen but, if alternative plans are made, the effects are reduced should the event occur.

Similar to other areas mentioned above, the risk register should be reviewed regularly and action taken on findings.

As with all risks, it is worth quantifying the costs of failure. This may be penalties for late or non delivery or costs incurred while receiving no income causing bankruptcy of the business. This approach can also help quantify risks and allow priorities to be set within the business.

Recognise resources required

Part of the business case and the project schedule will be the resources required, the largest of which is usually money. It is not true to say that with sufficient money anything can be achieved, as resources like time and skills can also be in short supply.

Going back to the project schedule, each task will need to be resourced and this is not just the man power. Office space, cost of 'phone calls, available telephone lines, stationery are all resources often overlooked.

When counting the cost of a project, all areas must be accounted for. Again, it is easy to assume that the good colour printer owned by the firm can be used to produce free of charge flyers. Nothing is free. There is the cost of toner, paper, wear and tear/contribution to lease, labour. If you went to the local printer, would it actually be cheaper? Their equipment is built to prepare thousand of copies at a time. Is the reason you are trying to do it in house so that you can change things? Is it that you don't want the content to be held to an external deadline? What is the difference between an internally set and externally set deadline? There should be none.

Staff are a limited resource. Never build overtime into a project. You may need to use it later and, if it is part of a schedule, there is no slack. If you work staff beyond a reasonable number of hours, their efficiency will reduce and their standard of work will diminish.

Make sure the funds are available. Don't waste time and money starting something you can't finish. It is disheartening as well as a waste. This comes back to the importance of a feasibility study and business case and the review of each. Again, as with risk assessment, ask whether you have the funds to continue. It may be practical to suspend a project or, if recognised early enough, source further finance to allow you to complete. Either way it is the benefit of continual monitoring that allows a choice of the ways forward.

Share the responsibility

The three main factors affecting any project are time, resources and quality. Resources are viewed as including budget. Each of these can be viewed as a side of a triangle. The reduction or extension of any one side has an effect on the other two if the area is to remain equal.

If there is a reduction in resource without an extension in time, quality will suffer. If there is a reduction in time, more resource will be required and so the change of one will be seen to have an effect on the other.

Anyone involved in a project will understand this interaction, not as a formula, but more as a result of real life. If you want staff to work faster, there is less opportunity for checking and therefore quality may fall.

The best people to help a project succeed are those that are working on a project. Through the desire of a successful outcome, people will put themselves out and almost work miracles. If they feel a responsibility and can see the benefit to them, they can ensure its success in spite of a poor manager.

Similarly, if those working on a project have no faith in its outcome, they will not communicate to help a successful outcome. If they understand the reason for the project and the deliverables and deadlines, the chance of success increases considerably.

Learn from experience

By sharing the project plan with others, you can often improve your chances of success. It may be they have worked on a similar project or they have a deeper knowledge in a particular area and can validate your assumptions.

It may be that the organisation has undertaken a similar project before and a post project review document was written. This will highlight the strengths and weaknesses of the approach taken last time.

In a similar way, both during and after a project, a lesson learned log should be kept. This can be anything from reliability of suppliers to conversion rate for sales calls. For implementation of software, it may be things to check during a parallel run. All these titbits can be logged and reviewed before similar projects are undertaken.

When staff raise the point that this didn't work last time so it won't work this time, open your ears and listen to what they viewed as the reasons why it didn't work. Even if you are about to take the same path as last time, it may only be the attitudes or recognition (financial or otherwise) that needs changing to ensure this is a successful project this time.

Who cares anyway?

If you don't care, you won't succeed. Going back to New Year's resolutions, wishes are easily expressed but it takes effort to make them a reality.

In any project there is always at least one person that cares. If there wasn't, it would not even have been started. Make sure that desire does not overtake reality. Because you care, make sure you share your passion with others so that they care as well.

Make it easy for everyone to care by ensuring they understand the goals, the deliverables and the path to achieve these.

Accept that plans will change on route but, if these changes are recognised and monitored, the goal can still be reached even if it has undergone a managed modification. It will end up as a better outcome if it is regularly reviewed during its progress.

By continual monitoring, there will be no shocks at the end, no nasty surprises and a good experience that can then be applied to other projects.

Remember, everything can be treated as a project. The project needs a clearly defined goal, a plan with stages, adequate resources, an open mind to risks and change and, most importantly, commitment.

Penny Lowe

Penny originally trained as an accountant and understands only too well the challenges of insufficient funding and costs of corrections. She has also spent eighteen years in the computer industry so has had plenty of opportunity to gain experience and learn from implementing many projects.

She believes that most parts of life can be quantified as a project and that without a clear goal you are much less likely to succeed. Penny now acts as a freelance manager helping business identify where they are trying to get and what they need to do to get there. She also teaches management as she enjoys sharing knowledge so that everyone can have a successful outcome.

Interview with
Charles Handy

What does success mean to you?

That's the sort of question I usually ask people. Well, I suppose it means two different things. A bit of it is being professionally successful. I used to see it as working for Shell, and success there was about moving up the ladder, until I realised that was rather a pointless exercise, since I wasn't ever going to get to the top so it would end in failure in a sense. Then of course when I started writing books, it was how many books you sold and getting good reviews and that sort of stuff. Then again, that passes with time and I suppose the much more important part of success, as I've grown older, is about being as true to myself as I can. It sounds a bit feeble really but as I've grown older, it's the more important one. Not pretending to be something that I'm not, not trying to impress people anymore, just trying to be me.

I keep on my desk a white stone. It reminds me of a verse I came across in the book of Revelations in the Bible, which said, 'To the one who prevails the angel said, I will give a white stone on which will be written a name, a name that will be known only to the one who receives it'. I think what that means is that once you discover what you're really about, and what you really are, and who you really are, then you will deserve your white stone. I'm working for this white stone on my desk actually, as a deeper meaning of success, which shall relate to my relationships with my family and my friends, and this sort of stuff. But of course there's always the other bit of success, somewhere in the background. Are the books selling? Does anybody read them? It gets less important as time goes on though.

I was 49 years old; I had two teenage kids and a mortgage to pay. I should have looked for a job, but actually, I think I ran out of bosses and organisations, quite honestly. Even when I was the boss I thought, 'well that's wonderful, all of these people working for me'. It turned out I was working for them! Finding the money to pay them etc. So with the encouragement of my wife, and I think this is very important, she said, 'why don't you do what you really want to do? You always said you wanted to be a writer, why don't you write full time?'. So, I had already got one book published, and I had a literary agent who came to lunch. He was not terribly excited at the idea that I was going to be depending on him for a future and he said I should not give up the day job, which is probably good advice when you're starting out, but I had to give up my day job anyway because I had come to the end of it.

With great trepidation really, I started on a chapter of my life which I had coined two years before. I called it 'the portfolio existence', where you had a collection of different bits of activity, some for money, some for love, some for necessity, some for the community, some for the home, and so on. You combine them all to make a fulfilling work life balance, I guess they call it these days. The trouble was that my work life was going to be desperately short of money. Writing books is tough you know. There are lovely moments where you go out to dinner with your publisher and she confirms the deal and writes you a letter confirming the details. That's wonderful, you've got a contract, you've got a title, and then the hard work actually starts.

I find there's usually about three false starts and you've got to dedicate yourself. You've got to shut yourself away. That's why we have a place in the country as well as a place in London, where nobody can interrupt. We shut ourselves away. Every morning at 8:30am to 1:30pm I'm alone, sitting staring at a blank piece of paper or blank computer screen desperately trying to think of something sensible to say, then coming down the next day and wiping it all off and starting it all over again. It takes two years to write a book in my experience. With the research, talking to people and so on and so forth. Yes, you've got to believe. I think everybody doing their own thing has a love/hate relationship with it. I can't believe that I'd ever be happy doing anything else. It doesn't mean I don't hate it when I sit there and I can't think of what to fill that screen with, but you have to do it, because that's what you do. That's your life.

You have to be passionate. It's not good if you want to be independent, thinking of some bright business idea and business plan to fill a niche. If you're not passionate about it, it won't work. The entrepreneurs we call the alchemists are people that create something out of nothing. The ones that we interviewed for a previous book, if they hadn't been passionate, if they were just there to make money it wouldn't have worked, they must really want to do this thing, they really want to put this product on the market. They really wanted to create this chain of shops and they believed that this was something very special that only they could do. Yes if it worked they'd make money, but that wasn't the point, because when they made the money, they did it all over again!

It's the same with books, if you don't want to write the book and don't care passionately that you have something to say, it won't work. Books take two years to write and three years to produce any income from. So I had to do something else whilst I was writing, so I did the odd appearances on company training programmes and that sort of thing; but for two years, when I was writing the book, it was pretty desperate. I had this postcard, money in money out, and desperately hoped the two would balance, which they seldom did.

I was rushing around the country working very hard and without my wife Elizabeth's support, it would have been very very difficult. Eventually, she took over what you might call my management and marketing function. It turned out the literary agent wasn't exactly good at raising

---

money or paying me large sums of money in advances. So Elizabeth became a brilliant brand manager for me really, because she said, quite rightly, 'if you're an independent worker, you have to become a brand'. People have to know you for your USP, your Unique Selling Proposition, what it is, how it distinguishes you from everybody else, and that requires you to appear occasionally. It also requires you to have a presence in the media. I was lucky enough to be invited to do Radio 4's 'Thought For The Day' on the BBC. That gave me a sort of presence in one area of the media.

The books then began to get published, I began to write articles in journals and so on, and so I became a sort of brand. It took a long time. One friend of mine said, 'how are you going to describe yourself?'. I was a professor, well a visiting professor at London Business School so I called myself The Professor but Elizabeth said, 'but you're not a professor, you're a past professor. Why don't you just call yourself by your name, Charles Handy?'. I said, 'well, it sounds a bit naked', and she replied that she had just been Elizabeth Handy all her life and it feels ok.

So, gradually I thought of myself as being just Charles Handy and began to develop a sort of public persona of some sort, but I have to say it really was five to seven years before it was established. The first years were hard and we survived and I was doing what I wanted to do. I sacrificed financial security and pensions for freedom and basically it was a very good bargain.

Charles Handy is an author/philosopher specialising in organisational behaviour and management. Among the ideas he has advanced are the "portfolio worker" and the "Shamrock Organization".

He has been rated among the Thinkers 50, the most influential living management thinkers. In 2001 he was second on this list, behind Peter Drucker, and in 2005 he was tenth.

Handy's business career started in marketing at Shell International. He was a co-founder of the London Business School in 1967 and left Shell to teach there in 1972.

When the Harvard Business Review had a special issue to mark their 50th Anniversary they asked Handy, Peter Drucker and Henry Mintzberg to write special articles.

||||||||||||||||||||||||||||||||||||||||||||||||||||||||||||||||||||||||||||

Watch this video interview plus many more like it through your free subscription to online business TV portal Expertsonline.tv available to you as a buyer of this book. Just send an e-mail to **info@expertsonline.tv**, *including the ISBN number, and the location of where you bought the book to receive your free subscription worth £50.*

Index

Symbols

R

S

T

U

V

W